Model Building and Finishing Guide

Model credits:

Chapter plates:		Figures:	
1,6,7	John Yarosh	6-2	Dennis Warner
2	Tim Warcup	6-4	George Etter
3	Mike Fritz	6-8	Mark Ford
4	Skip Samples	8-5	Dave Mason
5	Bryan Putnam		
8	Dave Mason	Additional models: John Yarosh	

Copyright © 1989 by The Testor Corporation
620 Buckbee Street
Rockford, IL 61104
An RPM Company

Text By Gordon McComb

Design and photography by Roy Ritola, Inc.
Art by Benjamin Dann
Production by BMR, Mill Valley, California

ISBN 0–938545–05–1

Table of Contents

THE ART AND SCIENCE OF PLASTIC MODELING

Anyone can build a model.

The prime ingredient is not the skill of the professional model master or a workshop full of expensive tools, but *patience*. If you take your time, there is no model that you can't build. Start off with a simple model and progress to others that are increasingly more intricate and complex. Before you know it, *you* are the professional master modeler.

To get from where you are now to that master modeler status, you have to start somewhere. And that somewhere is this book. The information packed between the covers of this book tells you everything you need to know to become an accomplished model builder. You can best learn by doing, and every chapter teaches you a little bit more about the art and science of plastic modeling. When you finish this book, you'll be a model maker apprentice, well on your way to being a master modeler.

There may be some initial frustration and disappointment, but the challenge, the excitement, the pleasure of working with your hands, the reward you feel inside when you have transformed an assortment of plastic parts into a complete, finished model, will make it all worthwhile. Building models is all of these things and more. Whether you are assembling a miniature replica of a car, truck, plane, tank, spaceship, or helicopter, model building brings with it hours of enjoyment.

About This Book

The Testor Model Building and Finishing Guide was written for the first–time model builder. It will also help people who have made a few models and want to improve upon basic skills. By following each project to its conclusion, you'll get better with each model you build.

The chapters are divided into main topics, like "Model Building with Cement," "Painting the Model," and "Adding Detail." The chapters should be read in order. You should not skip to a chapter later in the book unless you have some modeling experience. Each chapter builds on skills presented in earlier chapters, so you don't want to miss out on any good information.

You do not need to read this *whole* book before you start your first model. On the contrary, you can build a model for each chapter you read, as you read it! Most of the chapters present an "example" model that shows how the techniques presented in the text can be put to practical use.

You do not need to build the exact model shown in the chapter. A similar model will do just as well. Just make sure the model you choose does not have a lot more parts to assemble. Don't go over your head and try to build a more complex model than you are ready for.

An Introduction to Models and Model Types

Plastic models come in kit form and contain all the pieces required for assembly. Unless the model is specifically packaged otherwise, the box does not contain cement, paint, or tools. You must buy these separately. All of the tools and supplies you need are stocked by most hobby supply stores. If you can't find what you need at the store, ask.

Model parts are built to scale, and the scale can differ depending on the subject of the model. Most model cars, for example, are 1/24–scale, which means that every inch on the model is equal to 24 inches on the real thing. The unit of measurement can be anything—inches, centimeters, feet, yards, and so forth. The scale is simply a ratio.

Figures of people and military vehicles are often 1/35–scale. That makes the average staff car or tank six to seven inches in length—perfect proportions for hobby modeling. Aircraft are routinely available in either 1/48– or 1/72–scale. Even though the parts are bigger and therefore a little easier to handle, you should avoid the large and complex models until you have some experience. The extra large models are also the most expensive, so it's best to hold off on building one until you are ready for it.

Few models can be built in one sitting. This is especially true if you are painting the model. It takes time for the paint to dry, and trying to hurry the process will almost certainly lead to frustration and poor results. Plan on spending at least a couple of evenings building the average plastic model. Don't make it a contest to see how fast you can put the model together. You won't do as good a job.

A Note to Parents

Plastic model building develops skills in perception, patience, and pride in workmanship. These qualities should be encouraged, especially at a young age, for these skills, when properly developed, play an important role when the child grows to adulthood.

Modelers enjoy doing things with their hands, and tend to have greater manual dexterity than the average child. This won't automatically make your son or daughter a brain surgeon, but they will be more comfortable with mechanical objects. It's a rare modeler who isn't also handy around the house!

Perception is increased because the modeler learns to look for the "small things in life," the minute detail that gives objects true personality, shape, and form.

Even if you have no model building experience of you own, we urge you to build one or two kits with your child. You'll both learn while doing, and your child won't feel that he or she must do the job all alone. The biggest reason for abandoning the rewarding hobby of model building is lack of confidence.

Modeling is recommended for those age eight and up. If there are small children in the house, be sure the model kit and all related tools and supplies, are kept in a safe place. Models have many small parts, which if swallowed, could pose a danger of choking. Paints, paint thinners, and cements can be harmful if misused, and must be kept out of reach of small children.

Supervise the assembly of the model, and make sure that if the kit must be left partially unassembled, the remaining pieces are out of harm's way. Always store paint, paint thinner, cement, and other model–building chemicals in a safe place.

Enough talk. Time to get started. Get on your work overalls, grab your paint and hobby knife, and let's begin!

Chapter 1

*Your
First
Model*

There are many kinds of models available, from simple no–cement–needed kits to advanced models with hundreds of pieces. Some kits are harder to put together than others, so if you're just starting out in model building, your first project shouldn't be too difficult. A good model kit to start with is a snap–together car or truck. There is no cementing involved, and you don't even have to paint your model if you don't want to.

In this chapter, we'll show you the basic steps of building a Snaps-Together car. The model you build can be different, of course. The Snaps-Together car is an example so you can more easily see how to do it yourself.

For those of you who are interested, we will also show how to apply decals to the finished model and how to paint your model to obtain an even more professional look.

Figures 1–1 and 1–2 show the completed Snaps-Together kit. The first model is just the kit itself, without paint or decals. The second model has been given a quick 20–minute once–over with a few colors of paint and a couple of decals. When you are done with this chapter and if you take your time, you should be able to build either version. The unpainted car can be completed in about one evening. The painted/decaled car takes a little longer, because you must wait for the paint to dry. Plan on a couple of days to complete the painted version.

Figure 1–1

WHAT YOU'LL NEED

You don't really need anything other than your hands to build a Snaps–Together model. But if you want a better–than–average model when you're done, scout around the house and find two common manicuring tools: an emery board and fingernail clipper.

If you want to paint the model, you'll need a couple of jars of paint, a medium–sized paint brush (such as a number 2), and a bottle of paint thinner/brush cleaner. You also will need a small disposable aluminum baking tin or an old dish for the thinner/cleaner. If you would like to apply decals to the model, you will need a pair of

scissors to cut the decals you want from the sheet. Keep a few paper towels or facial tissues handy to wipe up spills and dry off parts.

READ THE INSTRUCTIONS FIRST

Every model kit comes with an instruction sheet. Some instruction sheets are more complex than others, but they all tell you the basic assembly procedures required to build the model piece by piece. Before actually building your model, however, carefully read the instruction sheet at least once. While you are reading, examine the parts of the model to familiarize yourself with the kit.

Take the runners of the plastic parts out of their protective bags, but do not remove the individual pieces. Some kit

Figure 1–2

Figure 1–3

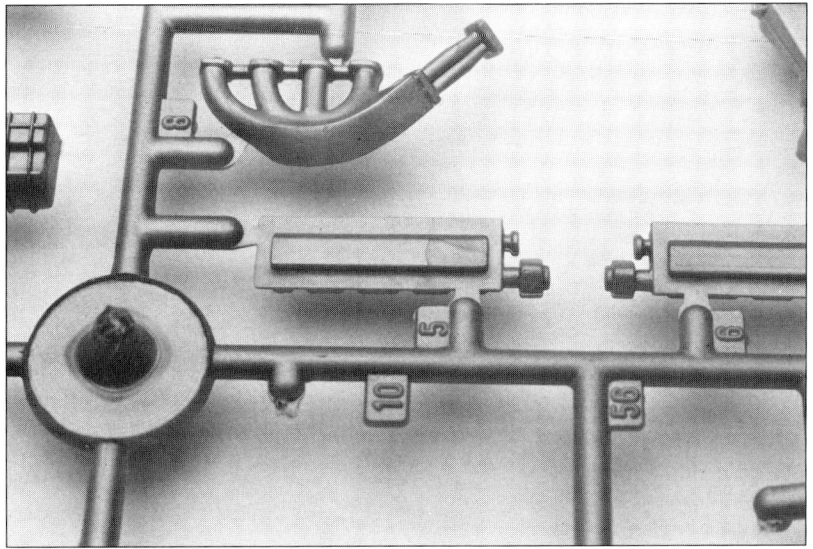

makers mark the part numbers on or near the parts. If you look closely, as shown in Figure 1–3, you'll see that near each part on the runner is a tab, and written on the tab is a number. This number corresponds to a part number on the instruction sheet and helps you identify the piece.

If you break all the parts off now, it will make it harder to tell them apart later.

STARTING THE KIT

When you feel you are familiar with the kit, lay the runners and instruction sheet on a table. You

may want to place a sheet or piece of old cardboard on the table, so you don't accidentally scratch the surface. Make sure you have enough light to read the instructions and put the model together. Some of the parts will be small, and if there is not enough light, you could make mistakes.

Following the exact steps in the instruction sheet, carefully remove the first parts from the runner. Do not remove any more pieces than necessary. If the instructions don't say you need a particular part for this step, don't take if off the runner yet.

With the runner in one hand, grasp the piece you want to take off with the other. Bend the piece back and forth until it snaps off. You should know that this isn't the best way to remove parts from the runner, but it's

Figure 1–4

Figure 1–5

the easiest and you don't need tools. In the next chapter, you'll learn a better way to remove the parts from the runner using a hobby knife or saw.

More than likely, there will be a small amount of extra plastic on the part. This plastic can be where the part was connected to the runner, or it can be caused by plastic that oozed out from the mold when the kit was made. This is commonly called "flash." Both kinds of extra plastic are shown in Figure 1–4.

Do not confuse flash or leftover runner plastic with the "locating pins" that are modeled into the joining edges of the pieces (see Figure 1–5). The stems or pins are meant to go into matching holes on another part. If you cut off or file the stems, your model may not fit together correctly. You especially need the stems in a Snaps-Together kit, or the pieces won't stay together!

Use the emery board to file away the flash. Go slowly and inspect your work every few strokes of the board. You can use the fingernail clippers to remove the nub of plastic left over from the connection to the runner. Carefully nibble the leftover plastic with the clipper a little bit at a time. The last speck of plastic can be smoothed away with the emery board.

While cutting or sanding, hold the part gently. If you apply too much pressure while holding the part, you may break it (a broken part can often be cemented back together, but it's easier to avoid breakage in the first place). If the part is too small to hold while cutting or sanding, place it on the table and work with it there. Avoid over-handling small parts. They are the easiest ones to break.

ASSEMBLING THE KIT

Now comes the fun part! Assemble the model as explained in the instructions. To put two pieces together, align the stems in the first piece with the holes in the other. Press the pieces together firmly but gently. Don't apply too much pressure or one of the pieces may break.

Don't jump ahead in the instructions. If you skip around, you may build the model in the wrong way, and other parts may not fit. Take your time and doublecheck your work now and then to make sure you are building the model properly. If a piece won't stay snapped on, you may have to cement it into place. See the next chapter on how to use model cement.

When the last part has been snapped into place, your model is done. Pat yourself on the back for a job well done.

FINISHING THE MODEL— PAINT

Your model may be molded with colored plastic, and you can leave the kit as is with its original color scheme. There is nothing wrong with that, especially if this is your first kit. Your model looks great as it is.

But if you want it to look even better, you can paint parts of the model. As you progress in your model–making skills, you will paint some of the parts before you assemble the kit. For the Snaps–Together model example, you paint the model after assembling the kit.

As shown in Figure 1–6, there are two types of model paints: those that come in small bottles and those that come in spray cans. Spray paint is used to cover large areas; it is usually used to paint parts before the kit is assembled or to paint sub–assemblies—complete sections of the model. Bottle paints are applied with a small brush, so they allow for more detail. We'll discuss only bottle paints in this chapter; spray painting is covered in Chapter 3.

Paints usually are not included in the model kit, so they must be purchased separately. Most of the better kits provide a list of suggested paint colors on the box of the model. You can save yourself some time by purchasing the paints when you buy the model. Refer to the list of the colors or look at the picture of the model on the box.

If you are just starting, you may want to get a plastic model finishing center or paint kit like the one in Figure 1–7. These come with a variety of popular paint colors. You will save some money by purchasing the paints as a set. You can always supplement the kit with a few additional bottles of paint in your favorite colors.

Handling Paint

Model paint comes in small glass bottles. The bottles are practically unbreakable, but don't test them by smashing them on the ground! Be careful when handling and storing your paints, and they will last a long time. Always keep the jars in a box, such as an empty shoe box or hobby center, and you won't have to worry about paint from a broken jar smearing the carpet. Most model paint is permanent. Once it is dry, it cannot be easily removed from most model surfaces without special solvents.

Open the bottle with your fingers or a jar cap opener. Once the bottle is open, set it in the shoe box, hobby center, or other container. Use a round toothpick to stir the paint gently. Make sure the toothpick goes all the way to the bottom of the bottle while you stir.

Why is stirring necessary? Over time, even the finest model paints separate, and stirring helps mix the ingredients again. Without stirring, the heavier part of the paint—the pigment

Figure 1–6

Figure 1–7

Figure 1–8

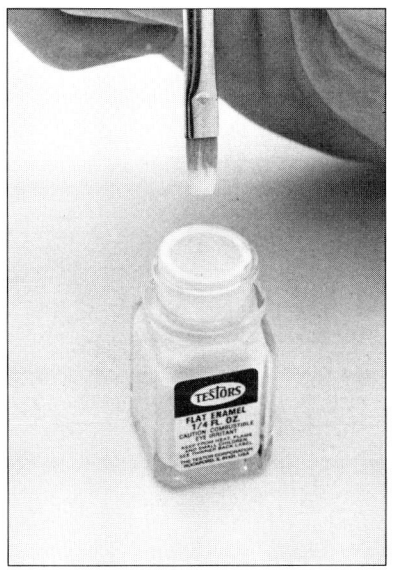

(or color)—will be at the bottom, and the paint at the top will be runny and thin.

Stir for about a minute and remove the toothpick. Scrape the toothpick against the inside rim of the jar to remove the excess paint. Use a new toothpick for each color.

Applying Paint

Hold the brush like a pencil and dip the tips of the bristles into the paint, as depicted in Figure 1–8. Don't dip the brush up to the metal collar. Over time, paint on the inside of the collar will ruin the brush. Through something called capillary action, paint dabbed to just the tip of the brush will be evenly distributed to the full length of all the bristles. Don't fight nature; let it work for you.

Brush the paint onto the model using straight, even strokes. Brush on the paint in one direction only, as shown in Figure 1–9. Don't go back and forth or side to side. Painting in one direction minimizes brush marks.

You've probably heard this suggestion before, but it's an important point to remember: It's better to paint your model with several thin coats than with one heavy coat. If one coat of paint doesn't cover the model well, let it dry completely (overnight), and brush on a second coat.

Letting the Paint Dry

Model paint sets up in less than one hour. That makes the paint dry to the touch (meaning that it won't leave wet paint on your fingers), but the paint still won't be completely dry. It takes from 6 to 12 hours for model paint to

Figure 1–9

During the initial one–hour setting time, the paint is still wet and tacky, and any dust that's in the air can settle and stick to the model. For the first hour or so, it's very important that the model be kept in a dust–free place. If you're working out in the garage, take your painted model inside where it is less dusty. Carry the model on a piece of cardboard; don't transport it with your hands.

Cleaning Up

When you're done painting, take a few moments to clean up and recap the bottles of paint. Be sure the caps are on tight or the paint will dry out. A tip: Storing the closed bottles upside down will reduce the loss of solvent when bottles are kept for long periods of time. Clean the brush using the paint thinner/brush cleaner.

To do this, pour a little bit of the fluid into a shallow pan or old dish (don't use a good dish), and dip the brush in it. Periodically remove the brush and wipe it clean with a paper towel. When it looks as if all the paint has been removed from the brush, dry the bristles and store it upright in a jar or glass. Avoid storing the brush lying down, and never stand a brush up so that it rests on its bristles.

FINISHING THE MODEL: DECALS

You can apply decals to the bare plastic surfaces of the model or over parts that you have painted. Unless you have painted your model with flat paint (as opposed to a gloss or semi–gloss paint), the process of applying the decal is the same for painted and unpainted models. You can expect good results

dry all the way. The drying time varies, depending on the humidity and temperature. Until you gain experience in painting models, you are better off waiting the full 12 hours—overnight—before handling your model. If you don't wait, you could ruin the paint job, and fixing it is really tough. Patience really pays off at this point.

if you take your time. In the text below, you'll learn the basics of applying decals. See Chapter 2 if you have painted your model with a flat paint. In later chapters, you'll learn how the pros do it and how to make your decals look even better.

The Anatomy of a Decal

Figure 1–10 shows a side view of a typical model kit decal. The decal itself is printed on a special film which is secured to a sheet of paper backing. When you apply decals, you use water to loosen the film from the paper sheet. Then you press the wet film against the surface of the model.

The adhesives applied during manufacture to the bottom of the film literally glue the decal to the model. Since the adhesive is already on the decal, you don't have to mess around with cement or glue. The adhesive also takes a few minutes to set, so you can slide the decal on the model to position it just the way you want it.

Preparing the Decal

Model kit decals come on one or two sheets of paper. Most decal sheets provide more decals than you can use. Some of the decals are alternates—you use some instead of others. Don't feel that just because you have the decal, you must apply it to your model.

Before you use a decal, you must cut it out using a pair of scissors or a hobby knife (use scissors for now). Be careful that you don't accidentally cut a decal in half. When cutting, it's all right to get the entire decal, not just the part with the ink. Get all the clear surrounding film as

Figure 1–10

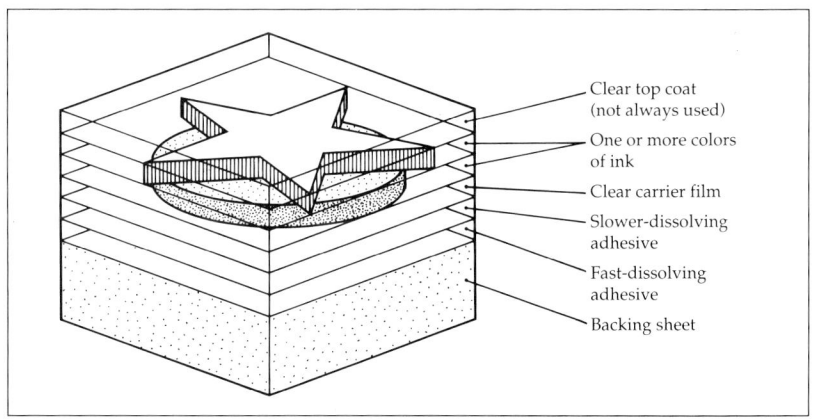

Clear top coat (not always used)

One or more colors of ink

Clear carrier film

Slower-dissolving adhesive

Fast-dissolving adhesive

Backing sheet

Figure 1–11

well. When the decal is applied to the model, the clear film will be nearly invisible.

When you have cut out all the decals you want to use, decide exactly where you want them. As a guide, you can use the decal placement illustrations on the instruction sheet, as well as the photos on the model box. But ultimately, it's up to you where the decals will finally be placed. Before actually applying any decals, place each one at the desired spot on the model. Does the decal look good there? Will it fit? Watch for sharp corners and curves. Until you're more experienced, it's far easier to apply decals to flat surfaces. For the time being, you should avoid applying decals to corners and curves.

Doing one at time, place a decal in a dish of clean water. You'll get the best results if the water is at room temperature or slightly warmer. Do not immerse decals in water that is hot or cold.

The decal film will start to separate from the paper backing within 30 to 60 seconds after it has been dunked in the water. Take the decal out of the water and place it on a paper towel for a minute or so. This lets the excess water drain from the decal, and it lets the adhesive on the film soften. If you leave the decal in the water too long, the film may separate from the backing all by itself. This makes the decal difficult to apply to the model. Whenever possible, do not leave the decal in the water for longer than a minute.

At this time, the decal film should slide off easily from the backing sheet, but don't do that yet. First, position the decal where you want it to appear, and gently slide the film off the paper and onto the model (see Figure 1–11). It's a good idea to "anchor" a tip of the decal film to the model before sliding it all off. Otherwise, the decal may fold up on itself, which may ruin it. Press the decal against the model as you slide the rest of the backing paper out from under it.

With your fingertips, dab the decal and surrounding area of the model with water. Now you can slide the decal on the model until you get it in the exact position you want. Do this as gently as possible. You will tear the decal if you use too much force.

When the decal is positioned just right, use your fingertips to press out gently any air bubbles trapped between the model and the decal. Start from the center of the decal and press outward. Soak up any excess water with a paper towel or facial tissue, but be careful that you don't leave behind any paper lint.

The decal will dry in 10 to 15 minutes, so you shouldn't touch it before then. If you are careful, you can apply additional decals to your model while the first decal is drying. Just be sure that you don't touch the ones you have already applied.

DISPLAYING YOUR MODEL

Models are meant to be displayed, not tossed into the

Figure 1–12

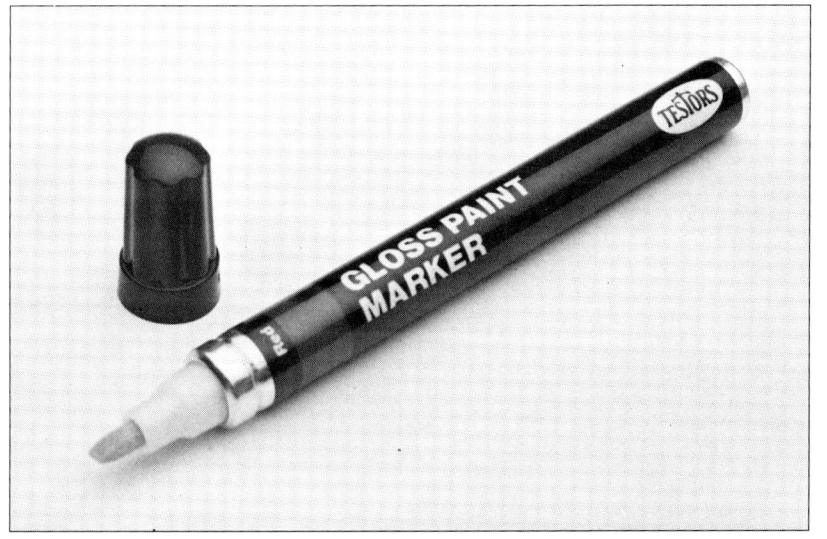

bedroom closet. A model car or truck doesn't need a display stand, but if you'd like, you can place the finished model on a piece of wood. Chapter 7 goes into more detail on building stands and displaying your models.

About the only thing to remember when displaying your model is to keep it away from heat and direct sunlight. Excessive heat will melt the plastic, of course, but even prolonged exposure to the heat of an air vent or the rays of the sun can cause the plastic of the model to become brittle.

Now that you've finished your first model, how about another? In the next chapter, you'll learn the technique of assembling a model using plastic cement, a better way to remove the plastic parts from the runner, the "right" way to apply decals, and more.

Using Paint Pens Instead of Bottled Paint

If you don't want to bother with bottled paints and brushes, an alternative is to use paint pens. A paint pen, shown in Figure 1–12, is like an ink marker: The paint and brush are one piece. You apply the paint as you do when drawing on a piece of paper with a marker. Paint pens come in most popular colors, including red, dark blue, light blue, green, gold, silver, and white.

Before you use the pen, shake it vigorously for two or three minutes. A mixing ball in the barrel of the pen helps to stir up the paint. The first time you use the pen the tip will be dry. Wet the tip with paint by pressing the tip gently against a piece of scrap paper. Keep pressing the tip against the paper until the paint oozes from the tip. You will also

need to repeat this from time to time while painting your model.

Apply the paint to the model in even, straight strokes, just like with a brush. The tip of the pen is made of a special fibrous material that can be cut with a knife to just about any shape desired. However, you'll probably want to keep the tip as it is until you gain more experience in using the pens.

When you are finished painting, simply return the cap to the pen. You don't need to clean anything. Be sure to recap the marker when you are finished, or the tip will dry out. If that happens, the pen may be ruined. If the tip has dried out, you can try to repair it by soaking it in paint thinner. Note that Testor paint thinner is recommended for Testor paint pens.

Chapter 2

Model
Building
Using
Cement

Most all plastic models use cement to hold the pieces together. Learning the right way to cement your models is the first big step to becoming a model master. In this chapter, you'll learn the ins and outs of using tube cement on your plastic models. (Details about how to use liquid cement that comes in bottles are covered in the next chapter.) You'll also learn some expert tips and techniques for improving your general model–building skills and the way to apply decals as the pros do for a super–realistic look.

We'll be using a Testor Stealth model airplane (see Figure 2–1) for the example in this chapter. Of course, you are free to use another model kit, but be sure it isn't too complex. The Stealth can be assembled in one or two evenings and is designed so that it doesn't require exterior painting. In fact, we won't even talk about painting the model in this chapter.

WHAT YOU'LL NEED

The prime ingredient for assembling your model is cement. You can use the stuff in the tube or in the marker pen. Both are shown in Figure 2–2. Tube cement comes in regular and nontoxic formulas. Both are excellent choices for any plastic model kit, but you'll find that the regular cement will hold the pieces together better. When using any cement, remember to cap the marker or tube. This prevents the cement from

Figure 2–1

Figure 2–2

drying out and clogging the tip. Before you start to build, go around the house and scrounge up some masking tape, rubber bands, and spring–type clothespins. These items will help you when cementing the model.

Proper removal of parts from the molding runners (or "trees") requires a few assorted tools: a hobby knife or a razor saw, some fine–grit sandpaper, and a sanding block (or small piece of wood). Use care when handling the knife and saw. These tools are sharp and can cut you.

Purchase an assortment of modeling sandpaper, such as Testor Hobby Sanding Films. The paper can be used when dry or wet and is designed to be used with plastic models. The Hobby Sanding Films assortment comes in five grades, from ultrafine to coarse. If you use regular sandpaper from the hardware store, buy the fine (280 to 400 grit) wet–dry kind. Cut the large sheets in fourths. If you have a set of miniature modeler or jeweler's files, you can use them instead of the sandpaper. DO NOT use woodworking or metalworking files. They are too big and too coarse for the small parts of the model.

The cement and knife or razor saw can damage tabletops, so add a hobby drop cloth and a piece of art board to your toolbox. You can buy art board at any picture frame or art supply store. To finish the model, assorted supplies you may need include a clear floor wax (like Future), a bottle each of Testor Glosscote and Dullcote, and a bottle of decal- setting solution. Read this chapter for details about how to use these tools and supplies.

YOUR WORK AREA

Serious modelers use a desk or table devoted to putting together their plastic kits. If you don't have a table you can use exclusively for your model–building efforts, at least try to find a table or desk in the house that is out of other people's way. As you build more sophisticated kits, you will have to leave the model for a day or two while the cement sets up and the paints and decals dry. If you use the kitchen table, you may have to clear it off come dinnertime, and handling the model may hurt it.

Use a chair made for the table, or at least adjust the chair so that the tabletop is about even with your elbows (while you're sitting down). If the lighting over the table is bad, bring in a desk lamp. Don't try to build your models in bad lighting. You'll hurt your eyes and you won't do a good job. Some of the cements and other chemicals you'll use to assemble and finish your model may give off harmful vapors, so be sure to work in a well–ventilated area. Open a window or turn on a fan to keep the air moving. If you feel yourself getting light–headed as you breathe the vapors from the cement or chemicals, stop and get some fresh air.

As you get better at building models, your collection of tools and supplies will increase. Keep them handy by placing them in a toolbox. A plastic fishing tackle box makes a good toolbox, with its many compartments and slide–out trays. The hobby center in Figure 2–3 is custom designed to keep your model–building accessories handy and in one place. The kit comes with an assortment of paints, paint brushes, sand paper, hobby knife, and other tools and supplies.

GETTING THE MODEL READY FOR ASSEMBLY

In the last chapter, you learned how to remove the parts of the kit from the plastic runner (or parts tree) by twisting them off. That's not really the best way to do it. A better method is to cut or saw the individual parts from the runner. Use the hobby knife or razor saw for this. Generally, the hobby knife is used to remove smaller parts; the razor saw is used to remove the large parts.

Remember! Remove each part from the runner as you build the model. Don't remove more parts than you'll use in the next assembly step or you may lose

Figure 2–3

19

Figure 2–4

track of the kit pieces and forget what goes where.

Using the Knife and Saw

To remove the parts, first place the artboard on your table and cover it with the hobby drop cloth. These coverings protect the tabletop from mars and scratches caused by the knife and saw. When cutting or sawing the parts off, lay the runner flat on the table. Don't hold the runner, because the knife may slip and cut your fingers.

Place the blade as close to the edge of the part as you can. Try to cut at the junction where the part attaches to the plastic stem of the runner, as shown in Figure 2–4.

- With a knife, press down hard to make a clean cut. Rock the knife back and forth while cutting.

- When using a razor saw, start the cut with a few light strokes. This makes a groove in the stem. Now press down harder on the saw and follow the groove to complete the cut.

If you have never used a knife or saw on a model kit before, practice on an unused portion of the runner. Pick a spot on the runner where the plastic is thin. That makes cutting easier.

"Prepping" the Parts

Most of the parts you remove from the runner will have little bits of plastic from the connecting stem still on them. Use the sandpaper or a small file to remove the excess plastic. Go easy when scraping the unwanted plastic. If you press down too hard, you may scrape the plastic off the part itself, causing a

Figure 2–5

As you remove and prep parts, "dry fit" them together to see how the pieces match up. Note the alignment pins that keep the parts lined up with one another. You'll use these pins for cementing. When you're satisfied that the parts fit together right, you're ready for cementing.

Using Tube Cement

If the tube of cement is new, it will still be sealed to prevent accidental leakage. Twist off the tube cap and use a pin to pierce a hole in the tip. The metal seal is thin so the pin will go in easily. After you've poked the hole, remove the pin and wipe away any cement. Be careful to not touch the tip of the cement tube or the pin. Cement will get on your fingers, and when you handle the model, it will rub off

big gouge where the part should be smooth.

File or sand off the occasional flash that may appear along the mold line of the parts. The flash is excess plastic that has oozed between the master molds during manufacture. Most flash is thin and easy to take off. If there is lots of flash, cut it away using the hobby knife. When cutting, it's better not to get too close to

the part, or you may nick it. Small amounts of flash that remain after cutting can be sanded away. In Chapter 4, you'll learn how to apply putty to cover up gouges and nicks, but it's easier to avoid them in the first place! Figure 2–5 shows a part before and after prepping. Notice how prepping removed the nicks made while cutting.

onto the plastic. The cement will eat away at the plastic and leave permanent fingerprints.

Squeeze out a little cement onto a paper towel. Squeeze gently or too much cement will ooze out. Practice squeezing the cement onto the paper towel until you can get just a drop to come out, like that in Figure 2–6 (shown with and without optional glue tip). Make the drop as small as you can, because for model building, the less cement you use the better.

Now try applying cement to the real thing. Pick up a part of the model that has locating pins (not holes). Dab the cement on each pin. Always use less cement than you think you need. Model cement is strong stuff and a little bit goes a long way.

If you get too much cement on a pin, place the edge of a paper towel against the drop of cement and let the towel soak up the excess. Don't wipe the cement off. You run the risk of wiping the excess cement against the surface of the model and ruining it.

Retrieve the mating part and align the two pieces together. Press them firmly to make good contact. Gently lay the pieces on the table and let the cement dry.

Using Marker Pen Cement

Cement that comes in a marker pen is easier to use than tube cement, but it isn't quite as strong. Be sure the tip is wet with cement before using it. Press the tip gently against a

Figure 2–6

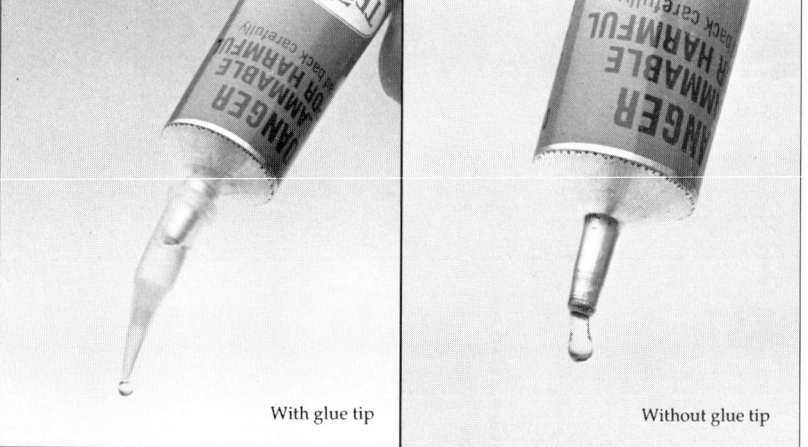

With glue tip

Without glue tip

piece of scrap paper to draw the cement from the inside to the tip. The cement should ooze out of the pen and onto the paper.

To apply cement, touch the tip of the marker against the alignment pins of the part. Through something called capillary action, the cement will transfer from the tip and onto the part. Once you have applied the cement, press the pieces together and set the assembly aside to dry.

Subassemblies

The first two or three minutes after applying cement is the most critical time for your model. If the parts are moved, the cemented joint may be disturbed. This weakens the joints and your model may fall apart later. So don't touch the parts for at least three minutes. Five minutes is even better.

But waiting five minutes between cementing each piece of your model would mean that your kit would take several days to finish. You can speed up the process by cementing the parts in subassemblies. In the manufacture of most products—such as cars, appliances, and toys—the individual pieces are first put together in sub–assemblies. The subassemblies are groups of parts that make building the product easier and more efficient.

The subassemblies of your model are small parts that go together as a group. You'd assemble the cockpit of an airplane as a subassembly, for example. You'd cement the chair, control panel, flight stick, and other parts as a group and set the subassembly aside to dry. As the cement is setting up and hardening, you can work on

another subassembly. When all the subassemblies are done, you put them together and your model is finished. Figure 2–7 shows several subassemblies that go into making a complete Stealth Fighter. No matter what model you build, you'll have similar subassemblies.

The instructions that come with better plastic kits show how to construct your model in sub–assembly fashion. With others, you must of think how the pieces fit together and which ones make good subassemblies.

FINISHING THE MODEL

Once all the parts are cemented, the model is finished. Or is it? Sure, all the parts of the kit are in place, but the model isn't really done. Most models are meant to be painted or at least given decals to make them look more authentic. Both take a little extra time but improve the appearance of the model considerably. In this chapter, instead of painting the model, we'll concentrate just on applying decals.

In Chapter 1, you learned the basics of applying decals to a model. There is nothing wrong with the simple approach presented in that chapter, but there is a better way to apply decals, one that almost guarantees outstanding–looking results.

Figure 2–7

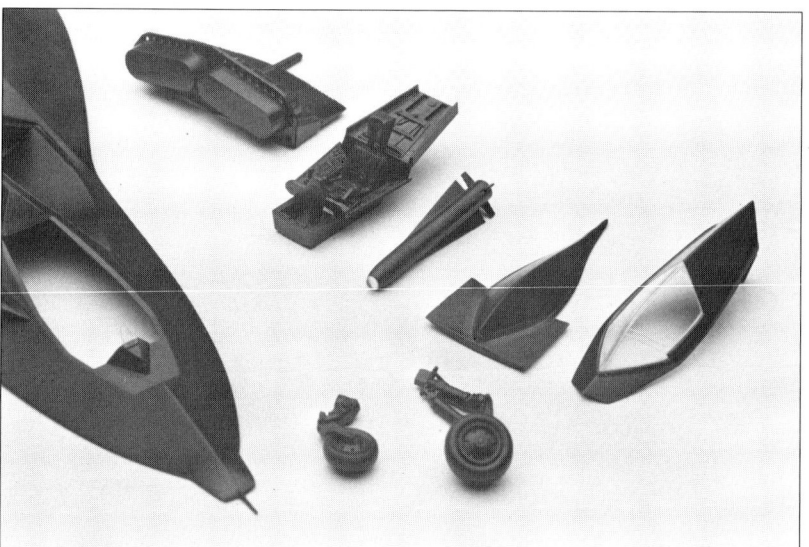

Washing the Model

Wash the model before applying any decals. Do this after the model cement has had sufficient time to dry—24 hours or longer. You can dunk the model in the sink and wash it with warm water (using dish detergent), or you can wipe it clean with a new sponge. Washing is an important step because decals and the various undercoatings we'll be using won't adhere to the surface of a model that has oil from your fingerprints.

Applying a Gloss Undercoat

Model decals don't stick on bare plastic very well, so you should first apply a light coat or two of clear primer lacquer, such as Testor Glosscote. Glosscote comes in bottles (see Figure 2–8) and is applied to the model with a broad tipped hobby

Figure 2–8

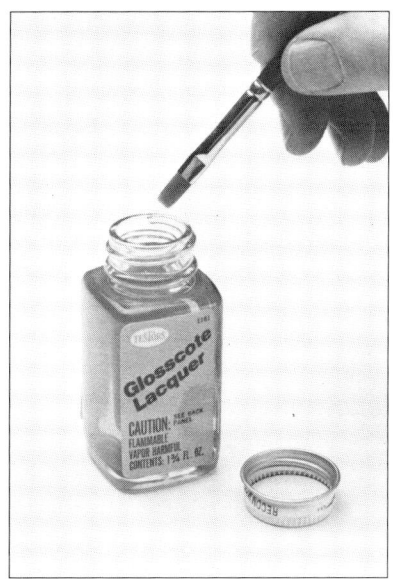

paint brush. Gently stir the contents of the bottle before using it.

As the Glosscote comes out of the bottle, it can be applied directly to the model, but you will probably desire a lighter coat.

Reduce it by mixing it with lacquer thinner (you can get small bottles at hobby stores). Pour some of the Glosscote in a small metal tin (the kind for frozen pot pies are good) and mix in a small amount of thinner. Stir with an ice cream stick. The consistency should be something on the order of pancake syrup—not too thin and not too thick.

Brush the entire model lightly with the Glosscote. Don't apply too much on one area or the lacquer may pile up and form a sticky puddle. Brush in one direction only. Any brush marks will even out as the Glosscote dries.

Let the Glosscote dry for 24 hours before applying the decals. Follow the instructions in Chapter 1 for cutting out the decals from the backing sheet and immersing them—one by one—in clean, clear water. Remove the decal from the water after 30 seconds and let the decal sit undisturbed on a paper towel for another minute.

Applying the Decal

To apply the decal, pick it up by the backing sheet and place the sheet and decal against the model. Push a wet cotton swab against the decal to keep it still. Now slide the paper backing away, as shown in Figure 2–9. It's always a good idea to slide the backing away rather than to slide the decal itself. There is less chance that the decal will rip or fold over on itself. If the decal is small, hold it by the paper backing with a pair of tweezers.

The decal will stick itself to the model. Use a dry cotton swab to soak up excess water from around the edges of the decal. If you can see a bubble in the

Figure 2–9

cause it is compatible with most all types of water–applied decals.

To use setting solution, take the decal out of the water and apply it to the model, as you did before. Once the decal is in place on the model, use a cotton swab to dab some setting solution gently onto the edges of the decal. Avoid touching the decal itself because it is now soft and easily damaged. Wait a few seconds, then soak up the excess water and setting solution from the edges of the decal with a dry swab (see Figure 2–10).

Figure 2–10

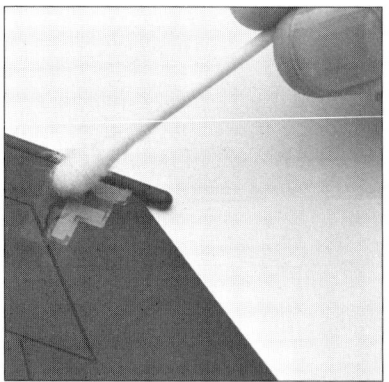

middle of the decal, smooth it out with a cotton swab moistened in water.

Using Decal Setting Solution

Some expert model builders like to use stuff called decal setting solution. The solution helps the decal form around the contours of the model. Testor #8804 Decal Set is a good setting solution be-

The setting solution may cause the decal to wrinkle up a bit as it dries. This is considered normal, and you shouldn't disturb the decal. If you have applied the decal correctly, the wrinkles will disappear after the drying is complete.

The Finishing Touch

Wait another 24 hours for the decals to dry and harden. If you look closely and hold the model in the light, you'll be able to see the shiny clear film of the decal. This is perfectly acceptable for a first kit, but if you want the model to look really topnotch, add another coat of Glosscote over the model and decals. The second coat will hide the shiny decal film and will give the model a uniform reflective appearance.

Figure 2–11

Glosscote makes the model look shiny. But most real–life planes and tanks aren't reflective. For a more subdued, realistic finish, use a flat lacquer spray, such as Testor Dullcote. Dullcote also comes in bottles, and it is applied just like Glosscote. Brush on a light coat, let it dry for 12 hours or so, then brush on another light coat. Before using the Dullcote, thin it to the proper consistency as you did the Glosscote.

An alternative to gloss or flat lacquer is to use common household floor wax, such as Future. Pour some of the floor wax into a shallow bowl. Dip a clean, lint-free cloth into the bowl and dampen it with the wax (don't get the cloth soaking wet). Being careful to steady the model by the edges only, apply the wax onto the model in even strokes. Brush only in one direc-

Figure 2–12

tion. For most models, this will be from the front to the back, as shown in Figure 2–11. You won't be able to apply an even coat to the entire model at one time because the wax will be wet. Do the model in sections as the wax dries (allow about 30 minutes to one hour).

Whether you use gloss or flat lacquer or floor wax, the last coat will help hide the decal edges, making them seem as if they were painted on the model. The final coat will also protect the model against the effects of age and keep the decals from withering or scraping off. If you use floor wax, keep the model away from sunlight, or the wax may yellow.

In Case of Trouble

Applying decals is an art in itself, and problems can and do crop up. But these problems don't have to be serious.

- Silvering. If the decals on your model have a silvery sheen, as shown in Figure 2–12, they are not clinging to the surface of the plastic very well. This can happen when you apply the decal to bare plastic or over plastic painted with a flat paint. You can eliminate the problem of silvering in the next model you do by spraying or brushing on Glosscote before applying the decal. Remember to wash the model before applying Glosscote.

- Bubbling. Air bubbles may get trapped under the decal when it is first applied to the model. You should always smooth the bubbles out as you press the decal in place (use a cotton swab instead of your finger and press gently to avoid ripping the decal). If you see bubbles after the decal is dry on the model, wet it again and use a pin to pierce the bubble (see Figure 2–13). Smooth out the decal and allow it to redry.

- Melting. Some decals may melt when submerged in decal setting solution, or the ink on the decal may run. Try diluting the setting solution or use another brand.

Testor Model Master Decal Set is compatible with almost all decals.

- Staining. White or reddish–brown mineral deposit stains may appear on or around decals after they have dried on the model. You can prevent the stains by absorbing excess water with a swab after the decal is applied. And you can clean the stains by wiping the area with a damp cloth or sponge. Make sure you remove the stains before applying the final clear coat of Glosscote, Dullcote, or floor wax. The stains will be permanent once covered.

- Tangling. Once the paper backing is removed from the decal, the decal film may fold over, sticking to itself. DON'T PANIC! Place the decal back into the water or setting solution. It will straighten itself out. Don't try to peel the decal apart with your fingers or with tweezers because you will only tear it.

- Chemical Reaction. Before applying any finishing lacquer to non-Testor decals on your model, first apply the lacquer to a non-significant decal to check for a chemical reaction. If you see no damage to the decal within 20

Figure 2-13

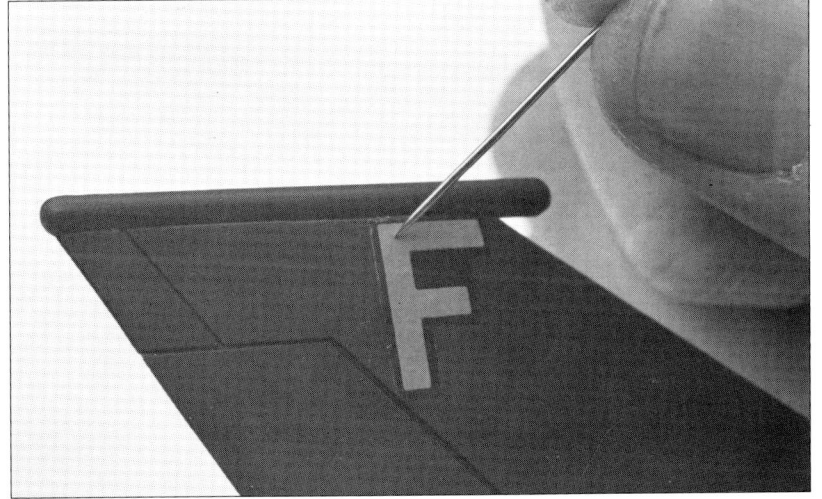

Figure 2–14

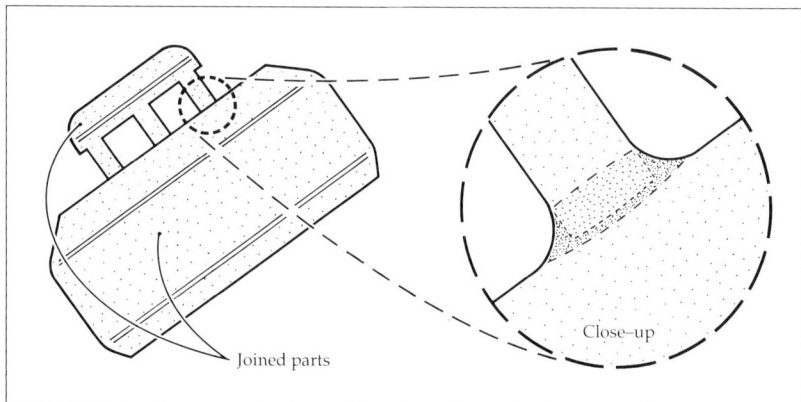

Joined parts

Close-up

minutes or after the lacquer has completely dried, proceed with finishing the model.

How Model Cement Works

What do model cement and plain household glue have in common? Not much, except that both are used to hold things together. Glue uses adhesives to stick parts together, the same way that chewing gum sticks two pieces of paper together. Model cement doesn't have any adhesive in it. In fact, model cement isn't even sticky when wet.

Model cement works by partially welding the plastic pieces. As depicted in Figure 2–14, the welded pieces then fuse together; in other words, they become one. The welding action creates a better bond between the joined pieces than glue does. But the welding also causes problems if the pieces are moved before the plastic has time to harden. The soft, newly welded plastic can become deformed if moved and the joint will be severely weakened.

If cement gets on your model where you don't want it, you should NOT try to wipe it up. That just spreads the stuff and causes more damage. Wait for the cement to dry and the plastic to reharden. Then sand down the cement and paint over it. Chapter 4 includes more details on fixing a problem like this.

Assembly Aids

You will need to hold the freshly cemented and joined

Figure 2–15

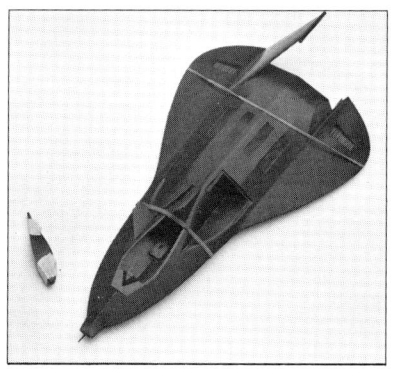

from the joints. If there is, leave it alone until it dries hard, then remove it with a hobby knife. Wrap some masking tape or rubber bands around the part to keep it together, as shown in Figure 2–15. Wait at least five or ten minutes before removing the tape or rubber bands. If any of the parts have been painted, use rubber bands instead of masking tape, or the paint may come off when you remove the tape.

model pieces together until the cement sets. That takes two or three minutes, even longer if the pieces are large. Instead of holding the pieces together with your fingers, use masking tape and rubber bands.

After you apply the cement and join the pieces, make sure that no excess cement is oozing out

Because of their size and design, wings on airplanes are best held together with spring-type clothespins. Attach the pins at several places around the wings to keep the halves together.

Chapter 3

*Painting
the
Model*

PAINTING THE MODEL

Painting is as much a part of model building as cementing the parts of the kit together. True, you don't have to paint every one of your models, but you'll enjoy the hobby of model building more if you do. Paint jobs can be simple or complex—you match the job to the model you're building and your skill level. Your first model paint job should be simple, using just a few colors. As you gain more experience in model building, the painting can be more complex, with additional colors, camouflaging, and masking.

In this chapter, you'll learn the basics of using both spray and bottle paints to add color and realism to your models. For the example, we'll use a Testor Ferrari GTO sports car model, shown in finished form in Figure 3–1. The kit is a little more difficult to assemble than a Snaps–Together model or the Stealth Fighter, shown in Chapters 1 and 2, but if you take your time and do the car in small "subassemblies," or sections, you'll be done in no time and the results will be fantastic. Advanced painting and finishing techniques are covered in greater detail in Chapters 4 and 5.

GETTING THINGS READY

As usual, unpack the pieces from the model carefully and make a note of the parts. Compare the parts trees with the instruction sheet (most sheets have a parts list or diagram). If any parts are missing, take the kit back to the store and get another one, or write to the model company and obtain replacements for the missing parts.

Figure 3–1

During manufacture of the model, a type of grease is used to help the parts trees separate from the master metal molds. This grease, called mold release compound, is still on the plastic and must be washed off before painting. Even if you don't paint every part in the kit, you should still wash all of the parts.

To prevent the small parts from separating from the parts trees, don't scrub the plastic to wash it; just immerse the trees in a sink full of warm water. Use a small dab of dish detergent in the water. Let them soak for a minute or so. You can help wash off stubborn release compound by gently stirring the water. Drain the sink and rinse the parts in cold running water (as in Figure 3–2). Be sure to keep the water cold because if you use hot water, the plastic will soften.

Place the wet trees on paper towels and let them dry for 15 or 20 minutes. While they are drying, turn the runners a couple of times and gently shake off any excess water. Remember: You can't paint or cement when the parts are wet, so be sure they are completely dry before starting to build. Also

Figure 3–2

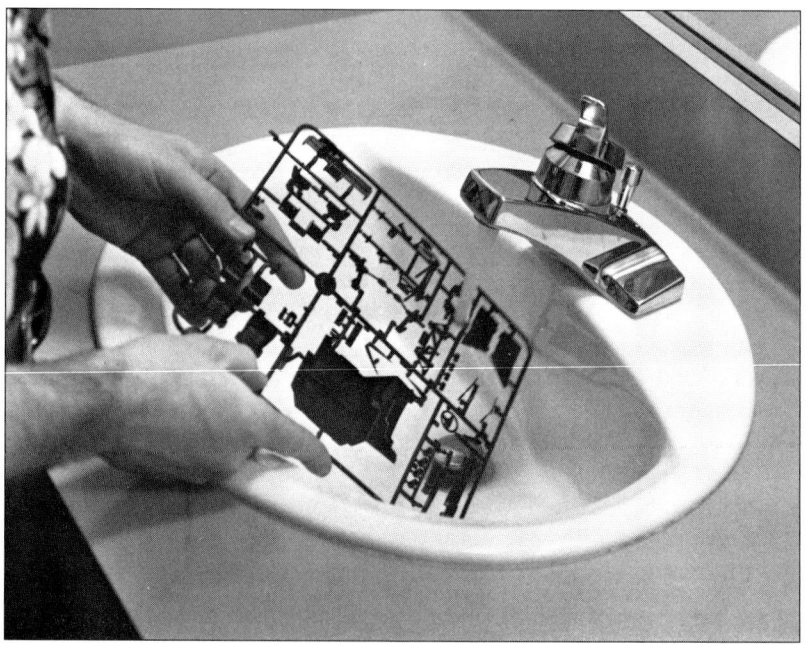

Figure 3–3

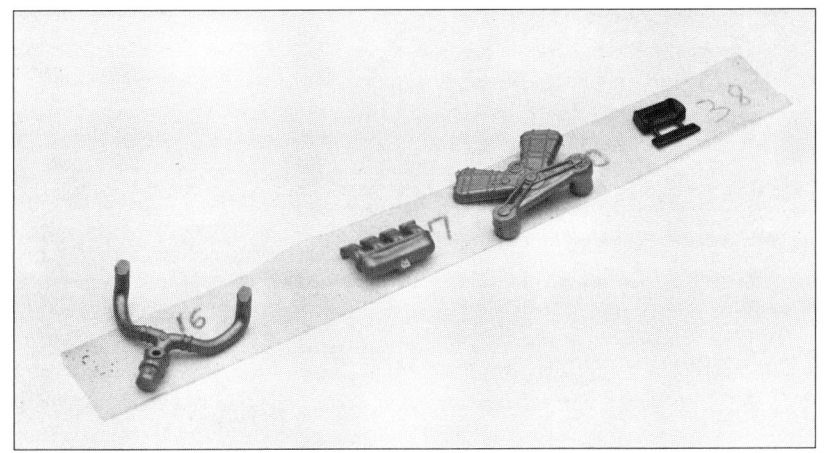

remember that your hands can leave oily deposits on the plastic, so avoid touching the parts as much as possible. Handle the parts trees by the edges.

After washing, carefully inspect each runner. If any parts have come off, collect them and stick them to the face of a strip of masking tape. Use the instruction sheet to identify the part. If the parts are numbered (they usually are), write down the number of the loose part beside it on the tape, as shown in Figure 3–3.

Carefully study the instruction sheet and the illustrations on the packaging box of the kit for the color scheme. You'll want the model to look as authentic as possible, so you should follow the suggested color schemes as much as you can. Experienced model builders often go to the library to look at books containing color paintings and photographs of the real thing (called the "prototype" by the experts). The prototype serves as the definitive or standard color guide for model building.

The color scheme can be more flexible when building model cars, because the real–life prototypes often come in various colors and are often customized by car dealers and car owners. Italian Red is a common color for Ferraris (and all sports cars), and that's how we'll paint the model in the example. You are free to choose another color, but make it a car color. Testor has a full line of metallic pearlescent car color paints. The paints are formulated just like the paint in real–life cars, and they come in a variety of colors.

Metallic car colors are really semi–transparent, so you'll need to apply a coat of primer to the car before the finish color. Without the primer coat, the finish coat will not have that opalescent and shimmering quality. Worse, the molded–in color (the color of the plastic parts) may show through the finish color. Applying the primer is a small but necessary step if you want the model to look right.

Figure 3–4

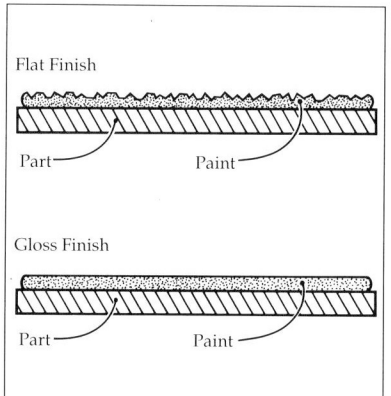

Flat Finish

Part   Paint

Gloss Finish

Part   Paint

A WORD ABOUT PAINT

In its simplest form, paint consists of a base and a pigment. The base is the liquid that lets you apply the paint to a surface so it can dry. The pigment is the color of the paint.

Hobby paints come in two general finishes: flat and gloss. Flat paint looks dull after it has dried, even when it is applied to a shiny surface. The dullness comes from the way the paint dries. If you were to look at the paint close up, you'd see that the surface is very rough. This roughness scatters the light when it hits the paint, so less light is reflected.

The surface of dried gloss paint is smooth, so light is reflected more evenly, like a mirror. That's why gloss paint looks shiny. A picture of the cross-section of the two paints is shown in Figure 3–4.

The choice of whether to use flat or gloss paint isn't always easy. Most cars use gloss paint, but only on the exterior and other parts that are supposed to look bright and shiny. You wouldn't want to use a gloss paint on the interior car seats, for example. Most car seats are vinyl or cloth, so they aren't very shiny. If you use a gloss paint for these parts, the model won't look very realistic.

Military models—planes, tanks, trucks, ships, and so forth—are almost never painted with gloss paint. A real plane, painted in gloss colors, would reflect light and the bad guys would spot it easily. If you plan on building and painting military models, use flat paints. U.S. Navy planes are often finished in gloss colors and are an exception to this general rule.

Generally, flat paints dry faster than gloss paints. See the drying chart in Appendix B for more information. Use the chart only as a guide. The weather, the thickness of the coat of paint, and other factors influence drying time, so you have to take these into consideration.

Most paint pigments are opaque, so once the paint is applied in a thick enough coat, the underlying color can't be seen. The darker the pigment, the more opaque it is. If you are painting yellow over a black background, you will have to apply several coats of paint before the black is completely covered up. But you will have to apply only one or two coats of black paint over a yellow background before the yellow disappears. This is the reason that if you are using many colors in your model, you should always paint the lighter colors first.

The pigments in metallic paints are transparent, so you can see right through them even when you apply several coats. As mentioned in the previous section, you will usually apply a light primer undercoat so that you see the true color of the finish coat, not the background. For special effects, you can try applying metallic and pearlescent paints over colored backgrounds. The result is an interesting mixture of colors—the translucent finish coat and a tinge of the background.

The small parts are usually easier to paint before you cement the model. If all or most of the parts on a runner are to be painted the same color, you can probably use a spray can to apply the paint. But if the parts are all different colors, or if some of the parts need special painting, you will have to use a brush to apply the paint.

THE PRIMER COAT

The primer coat will be applied with a spray can. The primer paint to use can be either gloss white or gray. Locate the chassis and exterior body pieces (those that will be painted Cherry Red) and set them on a large piece of cardboard. Be sure to shake the spray can for several minutes before using it. Outside, on a warm and windless day, spray the primer on the pieces.

Applying Paint with a Spray Can

The proper way to spray with a

40

Figure 3–5

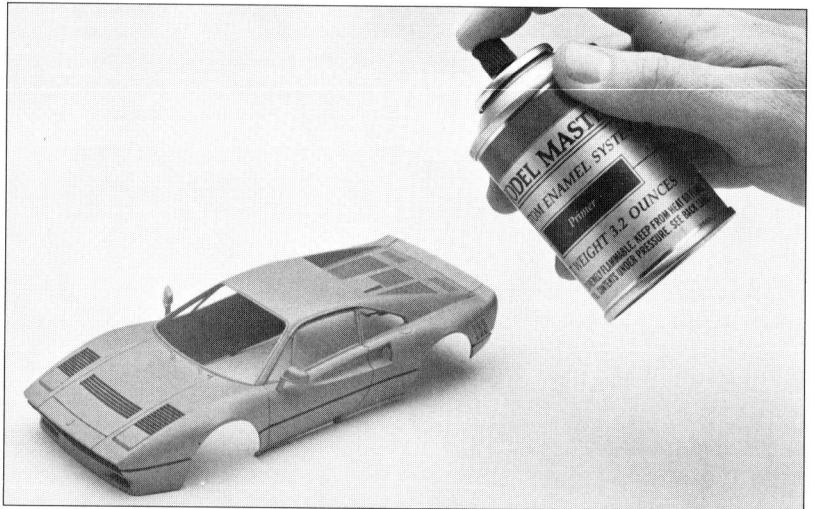

primer, so go lightly.

Let Dry

Let the primer coat dry thoroughly before handling the pieces. That will take about 24 hours, so put the pieces aside and concentrate on painting other parts of the model for awhile.

BRUSH PAINTING

Motor and interior pieces are usually small and require careful painting. For this model, it's acceptable to simplify the paint job and apply just one or two colors to the motor and interior pieces, even if the color scheme calls for more colors. You can apply the paint with a spray can or brush. Because the parts are small and may be next to other parts on the runner that will be painted a different color, you

spray can is to hold the nozzle 8 to 10 inches from the parts. Aim the can just past the piece to be sprayed. Press down on the spray button. The first squirt of paint will fall on the cardboard. Now, sweep the can from one end of the piece to the other, as shown in Figure 3–5. Move the can at a smooth and moderate pace. Don't go so slowly that the paint forms puddles when it hits the model and don't go so fast that only a faint wisp of paint appears. Don't release the spray button until you are past the piece. You may need to repeat the procedure several times to apply the paint adequately. You do not need a thick coating of

Figure 3–6

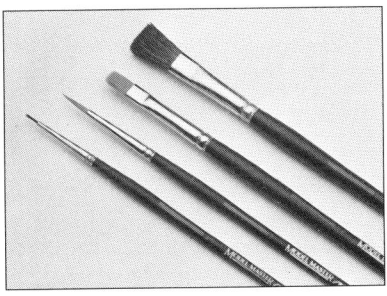

These are numbered 00, 000, and 0000. However, the smaller brushes are harder to use and control. For now, use a number 1 or 2 brush for painting the car model. As you get better at painting, you'll learn how to use the smaller brushes. If you need to paint a fairly large area, use a large-tipped brush.

Paint Bottles

Brush paint comes in small bottles. There are more bottled colors to choose from than spray can colors. Like spray cans, they are available in flat or gloss finishes. Choose the color and finish as indicated on the model's instruction sheet, or choose your own color scheme.

Open the bottle and use a clean toothpick to stir the paint. If the lid of the bottle won't come loose, use a pair of adjustable

plumber's pliers (sometimes called "water pump" pliers). Be careful not to use too much pressure on the lid or you'll bend it out of shape, making it even harder to remove. To reduce evaporation, pour only the amount of paint required for the project into a separate container. Recap the bottle after removing all excess paint from inside the cap and outer bottle rim and securely seal for long term storage.

Applying Paint with the Brush

To apply the paint, dip the bristles of the brush part way into the paint. Pull the brush out and gently wipe the bristles against the inside neck of the bottle. This gets rid of excess paint. Brush on the paint in even strokes. Go only one way. Don't brush it on in back and forth motions and don't criss-

should use a brush. Leave the parts on the runner for painting. This makes them easier to paint, and you don't have to hold the very small parts with tweezers.

Brush Sizes

Paint brushes for hobby modeling come in a variety of tip sizes, expressed as numbers. The numbering starts with 0 and goes up to 1, 2, 3, and so forth. The bigger the number, the larger the tip of the brush (see Figure 3–6). You can also get very small-tipped brushes.

cross the strokes. You may need to dab a bit of paint on the small detailed parts of the model to ensure even coverage.

Thinning Paint

The consistency of bottled paint is acceptable for direct application on the model, but you may want to thin the paint if it goes on too thick. (You can always tell if it's too thick because you'll see lots of brush marks that won't go away.) You need something to hold the thinned paint. You can use a disposable muffin or small pie tin, or the plastic palette that comes with the Testor hobby center kits.

Pour a small amount of paint into the tin or palette. Don't pour in too much or you will waste the paint. Open a bottle of fresh, unused thinner/brush cleaner. Use an eyedropper to pick up a few drops of thinner and squirt it into the paint; then stir it with a wooden stick. Keep adding more thinner until the paint is the consistency you want. Check the consistency by pulling the stick out of the paint. The paint should slowly drip off the stick. If it runs off quickly, it's too thin. If you add too much thinner, the paint will be too runny and will be hard to apply. It is much more difficult to thicken paint than it is to thin it, so add the thinner in small quantities until you get the right mix.

If you don't have an eyedropper handy, you can use a paper straw to add the thinner (some plastic straws will also work but beware of some straws that melt in the thinner!). Dip the straw partway into the thinner; then close up the top part with your finger, as shown in Figure 3–7. Being careful not to spill the thinner on anything, transfer the straw to the paint tin or palette. Release your finger and the thinner will come out of the straw. Don't put the straw too far into the thinner or you'll get too much. Just one or two drops at a time are all you need.

Changing Colors and Cleaning Up

Once you have completed one color, you can brush on the next. If you are applying multiple colors to the same pieces, make sure the first coat of paint is completely dry before adding the second color.

You can use the same brush to add the other colors, but the brush must be first cleaned. Pour some paint thinner/

Figure 3–7

cleaner into a disposable pie tin. You don't need much, just a few teaspoons. Swirl the paint brush in the cleaner and occasionally pull the brush out and wipe the bristles against a clean paper towel. Repeat until no more color can be seen on the paper

towel when you wipe the brush.

Follow the same procedure when cleaning brushes after you are done for the day. Store all brushes upright and make sure nothing touches the bristles. Otherwise, the bristles may bend as they dry, and the brush will be ruined.

FINISH COAT PAINT

The exterior of the car, including the body, bumper, hood, and other parts, are painted with the metallic Cherry Red spray paint. Apply the finish coat after the primer coat has dried. If the primer coat has not dried completely, the paints will run into one another and wreck the model.

Spray the finish coat as you did the primer coat. Be especially careful of airborne dust—you

don't want any flecks of dust settling on the car as the paint dries. When painting outdoors or in the garage (never spray paint inside the house), you can prevent dust particles from settling by using a "paint booth." This is merely a large cardboard box that acts to protect the model against dust and wind.

Place the model in the box and apply the spray. Cardboard is fairly dusty, so before painting use a spray bottle to wet down the inside of the box. Use a piece of coat hanger or other stiff wire to hang the model pieces (see Figure 3–8).

With all paints, but especially with spray paints, it is better to apply several thin coats rather than one thick coat. The paint job will look a lot nicer and the paint won't puddle up on any of the parts. The penalty of applying thin coats is that you have to wait for the paint to dry before respraying. Wait the usual 12 to 24 hours between coats and wipe down the model with a clean, lint-free cloth to get rid of any dust before you apply more coats. Experienced model builders like to use sticky "tac rags" for this. Tac rags are available at most lumber and hardware stores.

Figure 3–8

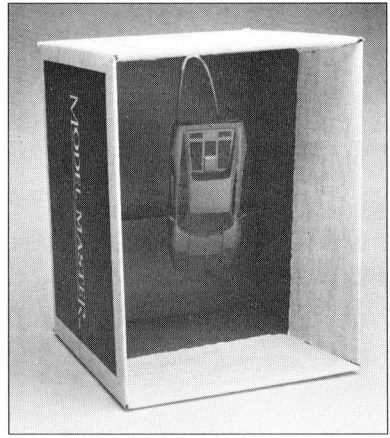

PREPARING AND CEMENTING THE PARTS

Let all of the painted parts dry completely before handling them. Even on a warm, dry day, it will take many hours for paint to dry and set up, so it's best to leave the painted parts overnight before attempting to assemble the model.

After the paint is dry, assemble the kit as indicated in the instruction manual. Remove the parts from the runners as discussed in Chapter 2. Model cement won't stick to parts that have been painted. Therefore, you will need to remove the paint from the cement joints prior to cementing. If you don't remove the paint, the cement will cause the paint to soften and you'll have a gooey mess.

You can remove the paint from

the joining surfaces of the parts in any of several ways. The easiest is to use a small file or piece of sandpaper. File or sand the piece until the paint is removed. Back the sandpaper with a small block of wood, as in Figure 3–9. Hold the paper in place with your fingers or attach the paper with double–stick tape.

Remember not to remove any of the plastic underneath the paint, especially if the mating joints must fit into one another snugly. If you take off too much plastic on an alignment pin, for example, it may fit sloppily into its mating hole, and the model won't be as strong. Go slowly.

Another way to remove the paint is with a technique called "adzing." With adzing, you scrape the excess paint off the part with a hobby knife, much the same way as you clean the

Figure 3–9

scales off fish with a fishing knife. You must be careful when using the adzing technique, because there is a chance that the knife can slip and cut your fingers. The duller the knife the better, so it's okay to use an old, worn–out blade.

To adze the paint off a part, cock the blade so that it's almost perpendicular to the surface of the piece. Apply light pressure and draw the blade toward you (see Figure 3–10). You will have

to go over the spot several times before all the paint is off. If the part is round, don't go over the same exact spot twice. Move the blade each time so you don't create a "flat"—an indentation caused by over–adzing.

If the pieces are large, you can remove the layer of paint with extra–fine steel wool. As with the other methods, avoid removing any of the plastic. Discard the steel wool when it becomes full of dry paint.

APPLYING CEMENT

With the parts painted and the paint from the joints removed, the model can now be assembled. You can use tube cement, or if you wish, liquid cement. Liquid cement comes in bottles and has a brush applicator in the cap.

Liquid cement is used a little bit differently from tube cement. Instead of applying the cement and then joining the parts, with liquid cement you join the parts then apply the cement. Holding the parts together with your fingers, rubber bands, or masking tape, touch the tip of the cement brush against the inside seam of the parts to be joined. Apply the cement at several places along the seam to provide many glue joints (see Figure 3–11). Capillary action will draw the cement into the seam and spread it along the parts.

Liquid cement should never be applied to painted surfaces because the paint will run. And you should always apply the cement to the inside of the parts (when possible), so any cement marks won't appear on the outside of the model.

Figure 3–10

GLUING CLEAR PLASTIC

For best results, tube and bottle cement should not be used to attach clear plastic parts to your model because the clear plastic may cloud up. Use ordinary white glue or fast drying 5–minute epoxy to glue clear plastic parts, like headlights and windshields, to your model. White glue is easier to use, but epoxy provides a stronger joint. If you think the model will be handled a lot, use epoxy; otherwise, you are safe with white glue.

Applying White Glue

To use white glue, squeeze a dab from the bottle onto a piece of paper. Take a toothpick and dip it into the glue. Touch the tip of the toothpick to the parts, being careful not to leave any gobs of glue. Press the plastic parts together and hold them until the glue sets. Or wrap masking tape or rubber bands around the parts to keep them together. If any glue oozes out of the joint, wipe it off with a clean paper towel. Unlike cement for plastic models, white glue does not damage plastic and can be successfully applied over painted surfaces.

Applying Epoxy

Epoxy comes in two tubes, usually labeled "A" and "B" or "1" and "2." You mix equal amounts from both tubes on a

Figure 3–11

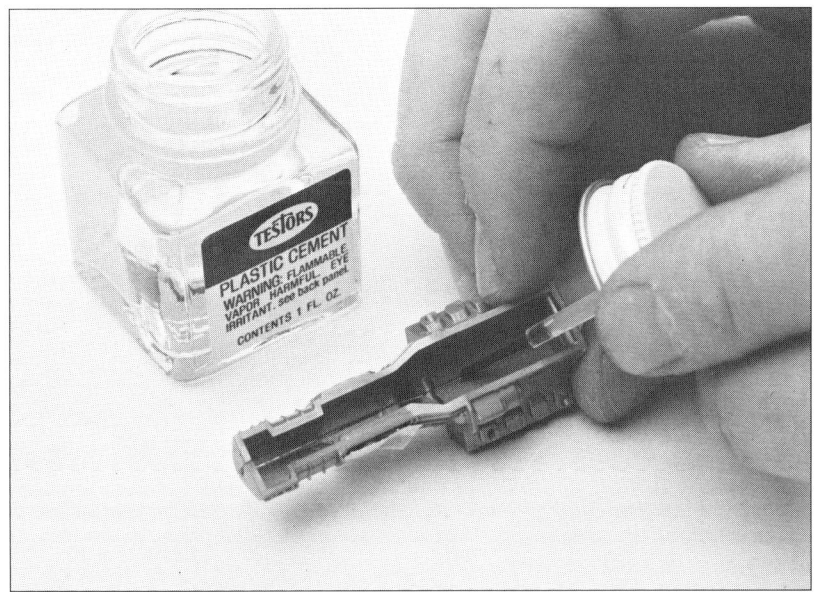

epoxy to the model. Unused mixed epoxy must be thrown away. You can't place the mixture in a bottle and store it for later use.

FINAL PAINTING AND TOUCH UP

You may wish to paint part of the kit as you build it. You may do so as long as you wait for the paint to dry before handling the parts. Once the model is built, use a brush to apply touch-up paint to those parts that need it. If there are any rough spots caused by excess cement or paint, use a piece of extra–fine steel wool to smooth out the blemish. Reapply another coat of paint with a small-tipped brush.

Decals can be successfully applied to any gloss finish paint, but you may want to apply Glosscote for an even smoother

piece of paper and then apply the mix to the clear plastic. The 5–minute epoxy popular with plastic modelers sets up in seconds and dries completely in five minutes. It also dries completely clear.

You apply epoxy the same as you do white glue, except that you must first mix epoxy together. Squeeze out an equal amount from each tube and swirl it together with a toothpick. After the two parts are thoroughly mixed, apply the surface. The smoother the surface, the better the decal will set. Follow the instructions given in the last chapter on how to apply decals. Remember to wait at least two or three days before applying decals to a painted model. You must be sure the paint is thoroughly dry and set.

Tips on Handling Small Parts

Small parts are best painted while still on the runner. Since you will probably paint many parts on the runner the same color, painting becomes easier

and more manageable. You can prop up the painted runner and let it dry, or you can hang it in the air. A bent paper clip attached to some string makes a good hanger.

Some parts don't come on a runner, or they may become separated from their runner, making painting more difficult. You can use a pair of ordinary tweezers to hold small parts. Avoid tweezers with teeth. The pressure of holding the part can cause the teeth to mark up the plastic. If you can't avoid tweezers with teeth, glue small strips of felt or cloth to the inside of the tweezers, to act as a kind of cushion for the part.

Your finger may grow tired of pinching the tweezers to hold the part in place. Another alternative is to use locking surgical forceps, like those in Figure

3–12. These are available from most retail and surplus hobby and industrial supply stores. The forceps are like giant tweezers and they are made with a ratchet–locking mechanism. Most forceps have teeth so you should cushion them with felt or cloth, too, as explained above.

You can use a number of other tools to hold parts for painting. A weighted soldering stand, often called a "third hand," has two alligator clips attached to a weighted base. You can place the part in one of the clips and use both hands for painting. Dental picks and tools, also available at most hobby and industrial outlets, let you hold parts for painting. If the part has a hole or crack in it, stick the end of the pick firmly into it. The design of the tool lets you easily rotate the part so that you can paint all of it.

Figure 3–12

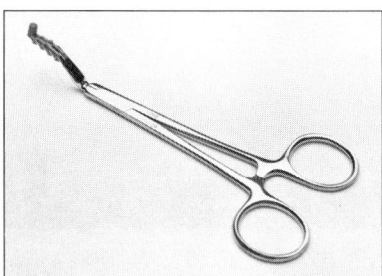

Chapter 4

Easy
Finishing
Techniques

Finishing is what you do to make your models look more professional and realistic. You've already done some finishing—applying decals, spraying and brushing on paints, even waxing your models with floor polish so they shine. If you've followed directions and taken your time, your models should start to look pretty good.

Now you're at that point, however, when you want your models to look even better. You want to smooth out the mold marks in the seams of your models; you want to spray primer coats so the paint job looks smooth and professional; and you want to apply finish coats for a long–lasting and protected paint job. Keep reading and you'll

find out how you can master these and other finishing techniques.

The example model we'll use for this chapter is a 1/72–scale Testor F–18 Hornet fighter jet, shown in Figure 4–1. This kit contains several dozen small and intricate parts. You should not attempt to build this model until you have had practice with other, easier kits, and you have read the previous chapters in this book.

FILLING AND SMOOTHING

Sometimes the parts of your kit may be damaged as they are removed from the runner, or they may not fit together exactly. There may be holes or unsightly gaps in the model, and no matter how nice the final paint job, your kit will look unprofessional.

Figure 4–1

Figure 4–2

Figure 4–3

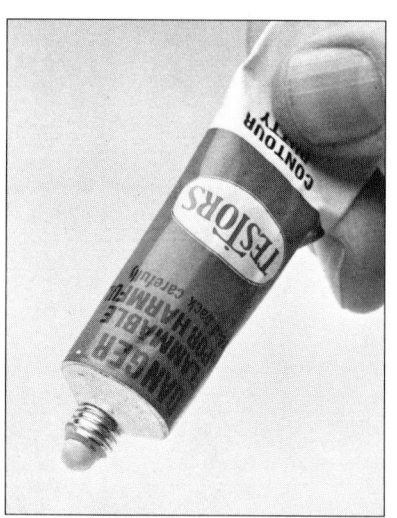

What is Model Putty?

Model putty comes in tubes (see Figure 4–3) and squeezes out just like cement. Out of the tube, model putty is fairly thick, about like toothpaste. You can apply the putty as is, or you can thin it with paint thinner. More about this in a bit.

Model putty is specially engineered to be used on plastic kits. It sticks to the plastic and won't harm it. You should never use wood putty or any other filler not designed for plastics. The putty may harm the plastic parts or may not dry to a smooth finish.

Applying Model Putty

You can apply model putty with the blade of a screwdriver, a toothpick, or better yet, with an artist's palette knife. You must work fairly fast because

Fortunately, all is not lost. You can use a special modeling putty to fill in the mistakes. Once the putty is dry, it can be sanded and painted over. If you do the job right, no one will ever know that you've applied putty to your model. As you become more experienced in model building, you'll use putty all the time to fill seams in joints and to make the surface of the model look smooth and unbroken, as shown in Figure 4–2. We'll practice this technique with the F–18 after learning how to use model putty.

the putty starts drying quickly.

Practice applying putty on a scrap piece of the model. The F–18 comes with an extra set of parts so that you can build the single–seat fighter or the tandem trainer. Assemble the kit in the version you want and use the extra parts for experimenting.

Figure 4–4

(As you build more models, you'll quickly learn to keep all parts you don't use; the extras may come in handy some day.)

Squeeze a small portion of putty onto a piece of paper. Don't use a paper towel because the lint will mix with the putty. Putty has a solvent base, so it can soak through the paper. Protect the table with a drop cloth and art board, as usual. Dip the palette knife into the putty and apply it on the part. Don't worry too much about neatness now.

Practice smoothing the putty along the length of the part. Use the palette knife. Try to get an even amount on the entire part, as shown in Figure 4–4. High spots will have to be sanded down, and that makes more work for you. Low spots will have to be refilled to make them

even with the rest of the putty. If the putty starts to set up before it is smooth, dip a cotton swab in a bottle of paint thinner and rewet the putty. Don't apply too much thinner or the putty may run. The layer of putty shouldn't be thicker than the thickness of your fingernail. Drying will take much longer if the layer of putty is extra thick.

Model putty takes about 24 hours to dry, so set the piece aside overnight. Work on the rest of the model to pass the time. Remember: Don't try to sand or paint the putty until it is thoroughly dry.

Sanding Putty

Once the putty is dry, it can be sanded and painted. Sanding is best accomplished with fine grit wet/dry sandpaper, used wet. If you have applied too much putty or haven't smoothed it out enough, you may want to use coarser paper or a small jeweler's file to get rid of the excess putty build-up. Do the final finishing with the fine grit sandpaper.

You will notice that model putty shrinks a tiny bit as it dries. As you gain experience with applying putty, you will know how much extra to put on so that when the putty shrinks, the hole or gap will be properly filled. If in doubt, apply the putty in layers, especially if the area to fill is large. The last layer should fill in any small areas left over from shrinkage.

You can test the smoothness of your sanding job by running your finger over the dry putty. Can you feel any hills and valleys? If so, keep sanding. If you sand off too much, you can always apply more putty and start over again.

Applying Putty to Your Model

Now that you have practiced applying putty on discarded parts, it's time for the real thing. The fuselage of the F–18 fighter (as well as almost any model airplane) is made up of two main parts: the right half and the left half. Where the two parts meet is a seam.

The manufacturers of the kit have made this seam as inconspicuous as possible, but it still shows if you look for it. On a first model, it's okay to leave the seam there. But as you get better at building model kits, you'll want to fill in the seam to make the fuselage look like one piece. After all, a real F–18 doesn't have a seam running down the length of the fuselage, so your model shouldn't either.

After the fuselage is assembled, and you have attached the wings, stabilizer, rudder, and other main components, you can apply putty to fill the seams. Follow the instructions provided above for squeezing the putty out of the tube and applying it a little bit at a time with a palette knife.

If you use an ice cream stick, use your hobby knife to cut the tip to make a spatula, as shown in Figure 4–5. Do the top half of the model first, smooth out the putty (before it dries), and then do the bottom half.

Figure 4–5

You really can't test how well you applied the putty until the model is painted. Once painted, you can see how the putty blends with the rest of the model. But you may not want to paint the entire model yet, so the next best thing is to apply a thin coat of gray or primer paint only to the puttied areas. You can spray or brush the paint onto the model. After the paint is dry, if you spot any roughness in the putty job, sand the paint away and smooth out the putty even more. Keep at it and you'll end up with a superb job where the seams between the parts will all but disappear completely.

Thinning Putty

Some cracks and crevices are too narrow to accept the full–bodied putty as it comes

Be careful that you don't apply too much putty on either side of the seam. The F–18 and most other airplane models have small bumps in the plastic that simulate rivets and the natural seams of the metal plates. You don't want to cover these up.

You can apply putty to other seams on the model, as well, but it's a good idea to wait for the first application of fuselage putty to dry before going too far.

Once the putty is dry, sand it down as explained in the section above. If it looks as if you need to fill in more gaps, go ahead and do it. When you're done, the putty will fill the seam neatly and evenly (see Figure 4–6), and you will not see or feel the hills and valleys.

out of the tube. Thin the putty by mixing it with a small amount of paint thinner. Squeeze some putty onto the paper and add a drop or two of thinner. Mix it with the ice cream stick or toothpick. Keep adding paint thinner until the putty is the consistency you want. The putty should not be too thin or it will run down the sides of the model when you apply it. Thinned putty takes longer to dry than non–thinned putty, so allow extra time before you sand and paint. You can store thinned putty for later use in a paint jar that's been thoroughly cleaned out.

Figure 4–6

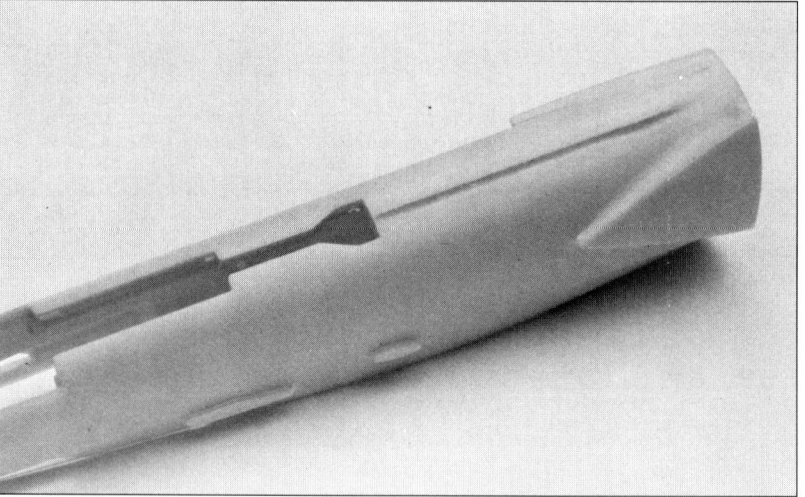

PRIMER PAINTING

In the last chapter, you learned about applying a coat of primer to the model before the actual painting. The primer step is not always necessary, but it helps your models have a smoother, more refined look. The primer also helps seal any putty you have applied to the model and locks out moisture. You'll especially need the primer if you are painting the model with a metallic or metal flake paint. These paints use transparent pigments, so the color of the model can show through the final coat of paint.

There are a variety of primers you can use, as well as a number of paints you can use as a primer. Real primer is called chromate or zinc chromate, and has a slightly green tint. This kind of paint does the best job at priming the model for subsequent painting. It is available from Testor in both bottle and spray form, and it has a flat finish.

You can also use Glosscote or Dullcote as the underpaint primer. Both Glosscote and Dullcote are lacquers, but they can be successfully applied under Testor enamel paint (usually, you don't want to mix lacquers and enamels). It comes in bottles and spray cans.

Neutral color paints can also be used as primers. White is a good choice if the final color is very light, like yellow. Rust, tan, and gray are also good choices because they do a good job of covering the plastic of the model, but they aren't so dark that they affect the finish paint. Obviously, you would not want to use black as a primer because it

would show through almost any color.

You can use either gloss or flat finish paint, but flat is probably the best all–around choice. Flat paint dries faster than gloss paint, and the rough finish helps the finish paint adhere better. If you want a really smooth final paint job, however, you should buff the primer with fine steel wool (000 or 0000)* before applying the finish coat. Buffing smooths the paint. Be sure to remove the paint dust before applying the finish coat, or bits of dried primer will show up on the finished model. Feel free to use steel wool between successive coats of the finish paint. That helps smooth out the final paint job, too.

* Steel wool that has been treated with oil is not suitable for this. Use only dry steel wool.

APPLYING PROTECTIVE OVERCOATS

In Chapter 2, you learned how to spread a thin layer of kitchen floor wax over the model. The wax adds a touch of brilliance to the finished kit and also helps protect its surface. A protective overcoat is especially important when you have painted the model or applied decals.

Testor Dullcote and Glosscote lacquers are the most common and long–lasting forms of overcoats. The easiest method to apply these is by spraying. Use Glosscote on models that should have a shiny finish (such as cars); Dullcote on everything else (especially military aircraft).

You may need to apply several coats to cover the model ade-

Figure 4–7

quately. If you apply too thick a coat, the lacquer will pool up in one area and look unsightly, as illustrated in Figure 4–7. After it has dried completely, use extra–fine steel wool to buff away the extra lacquer. Do the same for any bubbles you see in the finish. Respray a thin coat and let the model dry for at least 24 hours before handling it.

How the Weather Affects Paint Drying Time

Throughout this book, you've read how you should wait a certain number of hours for paint to dry. Most gloss finish paints take 12 to 24 hours to dry completely; flat finish paints take about half this time. Testor enamels take 24 hours to dry completely (both gloss and flat). Generally, lacquers dry much more quickly, usually within 1 hour, depending on the type of lacquer, thickness of coat, and whether the lacquer is applied by spray or brush. Testor putty should be allowed to dry for at least 24 hours before any wet or dry sanding is begun.

As you may have guessed, the weather partially determines how long paint, lacquer, or putty take to dry. In a warm, dry climate, drying time is very quick. But decrease the temperature or increase the humidity (the amount of moisture in the air), and drying time increases.

Appendixes A and B list the average drying times for Testor paints, lacquers, putties, and cements. As you can see from the charts, changes in temperature and humidity affect the drying time, especially for paints. For example, you should wait another 12 hours for paint to dry if the humidity is above 50 percent and 24 more hours if the humidity is above 80 percent. You can find out the humidity with a dial hygrometer (which is like a thermometer, only it registers moisture content in the air), or by checking the daily newspaper.

Some weather just isn't well suited for model building, but that doesn't mean you have to give up your hobby just because it's raining outside. You can help speed up the drying process with the use of a hair blow dryer. Set the dryer on low or no heat and point it at the model. Keep the nozzle of the dryer at least six inches away from the model, as shown in Figure 4–8.

Turn on the switch and let the rush of air speed–dry the paint. Remember to use as little heat as possible, or you may ruin the model. Keep the dryer moving at all times so that the paint dries evenly. This technique is not recommended for high-gloss finishes (auto bodies).

Figure 4–8

Chapter 5

Adding
Detail

In model building, it's the small things that count. Realism is best achieved by adding a few important details. Rather than trying to make every little part of the model look exactly like the real thing—which is beyond even the best model builder—you spend extra time adding detail to critical parts of the model, such as:

- The camouflage paint job of a World War II tank.
- The nicks around the propeller and leading edge of an airplane.
- Diesel soot from the stacks of a Korean War–era battleship.
- Fuel spills and evidence of "hurried" repairs in a helicopter gunship.

These are just some of the details you can add to your models. We'll talk about these and other effects in this chapter, and how you can duplicate the techniques in your models. The example kit in this chapter is the Vought F4U–1D Corsair, a single–engine World War II fighter that saw considerable action in the Pacific. This 1/72–scale model is moderately easy to assemble and comes with a variety of parts that beg for an accurate detail job: the underwing bombs, the landing gear, and the cockpit canopy. The model is shown, assembled and detailed, in Figure 5–1.

Figure 5–1

STUDYING THE F4U–1D CORSAIR

A lot has been written about the F4U. Before you attempt building yours, why don't you take a trip to the library and look up the history of this aircraft? Study the color scheme and markings. Try to find photos of actual aircraft, not just artist's drawings. The photos may show how the plane looked after a few missions in and around the islands of the Pacific. If you're lucky enough, you may even be able to find a restored F4U at a local municipal airport or airplane museum. The F4U is considered a collector's item, and airplane buffs are fond of collecting and restoring them.

Whether you have researched the model in the library or in person at an airport or museum, keep your eyes out for the small things—the details. Rather than trying to take in the plane as a whole or digest every tiny aspect, concentrate on major points of interest and visualize how these might look in miniature.

What does the cockpit look like through the canopy? Is the cockpit full of colorful dials and controls, or it fairly colorless and simple? You'll want to duplicate it, as closely as possible, in your finished model. The cockpit is an integral part of the plane, so don't overlook it.

Now closely study the wheels and landing gear. If the plane saw any action at all and hasn't been restored to "showroom" condition, the tires will be bald or nearly bald. Now note the color scheme of the landing gear. There are a number of colors, including silver from bare metal parts. Try to duplicate this color scheme as closely as possible in your model. Think how drab the model would look if you painted the landing gear all one color.

Finally, look at the markings—the numbers and insignias—that you will reproduce in your model with decals. Note their positions and how they look after wear. Some of the numbers and insignias may be chipped and worn off. There is nothing stopping you from duplicating this effect with your decals. By the way, if the decals included with the model don't suit your fancy, you can always purchase additional sheets at a hobby store. Most stores have a wide variety, and you can choose the exact markings you want for your model.

Now, time to get to work!

PAINTING AND DETAILING SMALL PARTS

Detail is best conveyed through variations in color. A model painted all one color looks far less realistic than a model carefully painted in many colors. Note the word "carefully." It will not do for you to paint parts of your model indiscriminately in whatever color you choose. Your paint job must be as close to the prototype as possible, or the model will look fake.

Figure 5–2

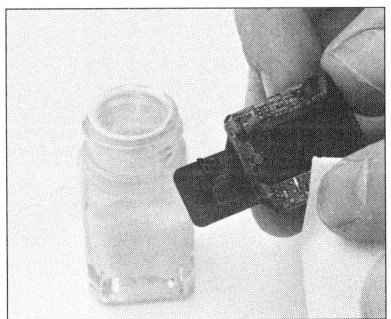

Painting the Cockpit

The cockpit is generally assembled first in almost any airplane kit, so it is the first sub–assembly that requires your attention. Paint the individual pieces as usual and assemble them after they have dried. If the model came with decals for the cockpit dials and controls, apply them.

If the cockpit has molded–in details for the gauges and other components, you can paint them with a light–colored paint (usually white). It's almost impossible to paint individually every small switch, gauge, and needle, and make them look good, so just try for an overall effect.

With a bit of practice, however, you can color just the molded–in raised detail. You can do it in two ways: either apply white

paint over black or black paint over white.

For the first method, paint the cockpit black (or gray or some other color as dictated in the color scheme instructions that came with the model). Let the paint dry. Fold a piece of linen or cotton (from a discarded sheet, for example) into a small 1– or 2–inch square.

Dip one side of it in white paint and then scrape as much of the paint back into the bottle as you can. The cloth should have paint in it, but the paint should not be runny. Gently rub the fabric against the cockpit. If you are careful, you can apply color only to the raised portions of the cockpit, as shown in Figure 5–2. If you smear some paint on the lower portions, quickly wipe it off and try again.

You won't deposit much paint on the raised portion of the cockpit, and the paint may not go on evenly. But the overall effect should look realistic when the entire model is finished.

The other method achieves the effect in reverse. Paint the cockpit white and let it dry. Now paint the background color (black, gray, or whatever) over the entire cockpit. As quickly as possible, scrape the front surface of the cockpit against a clean piece of linen.

As long as the background paint has not had a chance to dry, you will rub it off the raised portions of the cockpit, revealing the white paint underneath. Again, the raised portions won't be completely white, but it's the overall effect you are after. If you don't like the way it looks the first time around, repaint the cockpit and start over.

Painting the Landing Gear

The landing gear is another sub–assembly of aircraft models that requires extra attention. Landing gear parts are small, especially in a 1/72–scale kit like the F4U, so handle them carefully. For extra strength, you may want to glue them to the fuselage with 5–minute epoxy. Model cement softens the plastic of the landing gear and can considerably weaken it.

Remember to follow the assembly directions carefully if the landing gear is the type that folds up. If you cement a part by mistake that shouldn't be cemented, the landing gear won't function as it should. The same goes for the propellers of airplanes, the blades of helicopters, and the doors, trunk, and hood of model cars.

Follow the painting instructions included with the kit for the colors to use on the various landing gear parts. Some parts are bare metal; use silver or chrome paint for these, as shown in Figure 5–3. Be sure that the previous coat of paint has dried completely before applying another coat or color. To avoid any possibility of lifting (wrinkling), you should overcoat within 3 hours or after 16 hours of the application of the first coat. If you don't wait long enough, the paints may run into one another or become so thin that they sag. In both cases, your model will be ruined, and the only way to fix it is to remove the paint completely and start over.

Figure 5–3

Canopies are not made of one solid piece of glass. They are composed of many pieces of glass assembled in a frame. The frame of the model's canopy is molded into the plastic, but it needs to be brought out if you want to add detail.

It is nearly impossible to paint the frame lines of the canopy by hand. The pros have several other ways of doing it. You can experiment with the method you like best, or even come up with your own. As long as the end result looks authentic, any technique you use is the "right way" to do it.

Adding Detail to Canopies and Canopy Frames

The F4U kit, as well as most airplane models, comes with a clear plastic piece for the canopy window. In previous chapters, you've already learned how to attach the canopy to the model without clouding the clear plastic. Nevertheless, the canopy of a real airplane, especially one of World War II vintage, is not clear.

Figure 5–4

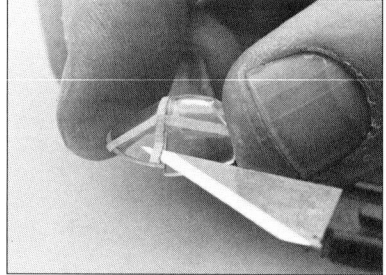

Figure 5–5

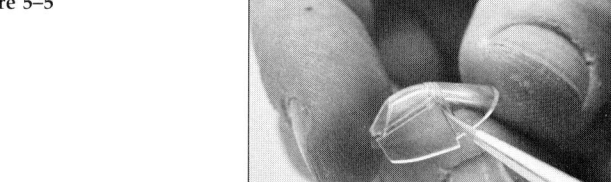

Perhaps the easiest way to add detail to the frame lines of the canopy is to use graphic arts tape. This tape is available at art supply stores, and comes in various colors, widths, and finishes. The roll will last you for many, many models. The 1/32– or 1/16–inch– wide tape, in flat white, gray, or light brown, does the trick nicely.

To apply the tape, cut out a small portion with a hobby knife. Make the piece long enough to cover one of the pieces of frame in the canopy. Holding the tape by the blade of the knife, place it on the canopy, over the frame, as shown in Figure 5–4. Press it into place; then trim it carefully with the knife for a perfect fit.

Repeat the procedure until all of the frame has been covered. Incidentally, use only flat finish tape, not gloss finish. Gloss finish tapes are coated with a thin layer of shiny plastic, which can peel off after a time.

A more difficult, but far more realistic, approach is to paint the frame after it has been masked. A masking fluid, available at hobby stores, is first applied to the canopy. Brush it on with a number 2 or 3 brush (see detail shown in Figure 5–5). When the fluid dries, it turns into a thin layer of pliable latex. With your hobby knife, carefully cut around the frame of the canopy, peeling the masking from the frame. Leave the mask over the glass portions of the canopy.

When the framework has been exposed, you can apply the paint using a brush or spray can. When spray painting, keep the can some distance from the canopy. If you hold the can too close, the pressure of the paint could cause some of the color to bleed under the mask. Let the paint dry completely; then peel off the rest of the mask. You can remove paint on the canopy glass by scraping it carefully with your knife.

Adding Detail to Tires

Tires in model kits are either plastic or rubber. Rubber wheels look more authentic, but you can make do with the plastic kind just as well. Paint the hubs as instructed, but don't attach the tires yet. You can add wear to the tires by sanding down the surface with a piece of medium–grit sandpaper (wet the sandpaper for best results).

Only brand–new tires are jet black; all tires become gray when exposed to dirt and air. There is no suitable pre–mixed "worn tire" paint on the market, but you can make some yourself. Pour a bit of black paint onto a mixing palette or into a disposable bowl. Sprinkle a touch of talcum or foot powder into the paint and mix well. Keep adding the powder until the color is a dull gray black. Paint the tires and let them dry. Figure 5–6 shows how this simple paint effect improves the authenticity of the plane's wheels.

For an even better effect, press out the tires to make them look as if they are sagging under the weight of the plane. Here's how: Use an old clothes iron on medium heat and let it warm up. Position a piece of wax paper over the bottom of the iron.

Now carefully grasp the wheel and press it against the wax-papered bottom of the iron. Hold it there for a few seconds, then pull the tire away and see if the plastic or rubber has flattened out in the heat. Be careful that you don't burn yourself. *

You may have to repeat the procedure a few times until you get the effect you want. The tire in Figure 5–7 seems to have the right amount of "flatness." When you're done, turn the iron off, let it cool completely, and then remove the wax left from the wax paper on the iron with an iron cleaner. An alternate method is to sand the tires flat on sandpaper taped to a flat surface.

*Parental supervision advised for young modelers

Figure 5–6

Figure 5–7

Engine Detail

As with many fighters in the World War II era, the F4U aircraft has a radial piston engine. The bulk of the engine is under a cowling, but the cooling fins of the pistons can be seen through the cowling behind the propeller.

The cowling can be made so that it comes off, in case you want to display the engine. If you don't paint the entire engine, at least paint the front part. The engine should be painted a dull silver gray. Testor Steel or Aluminum paints should do the trick. Add detail to the cooling fins of the pistons by adding a touch of thinned black paint. Wipe the excess from the outside of the engine.

CAMOUFLAGING TECHNIQUES

The F4U Corsair saw service over the Pacific Ocean and was not known to be painted in camouflage colors. This section on camouflaging really doesn't apply to the F4U, although there is nothing stopping you from painting your model in camouflage.

Rather, use the information that follows for your other kits that should be painted in camouflage, such as helicopter gunships, tanks, and artillery and troop vehicles. Of course, some airplanes are painted in camouflage, such as the World War II Focke–Wulf FW–190A/F, Republic P-47D Thunderbolt, and numerous Japanese fighters. Check the color scheme in the instruction sheet that came with the model, or better yet, do research in books, museums, and airports to find out how the real thing was painted.

Sponge Painting

Perhaps the easiest way to add camouflage to a model is with a sponge. The effect is a spotted or stippled look that accurately reflects the paint job given to many military vehicles and aircraft, including the Messerschmitt Bf 109 and Heinkel He 219.

Sponge painting is easy: First paint the background color and let it dry. Thoroughly wash a new, unused kitchen sponge. Use detergent to get rid of the softener added to new sponges. Let the sponge dry in the sun; then tear off a few postage–stamp–sized pieces.

Pour the camouflage paint into a shallow bowl or disposable dish and dip the sponge into it. Blot the excess paint onto a paper towel; then dab the sponge on the model, as shown in Figure 5–8, depositing the paint as you go. When the camouflage paint gets too light, dip it back into the paint, blot the excess, and continue painting.

You will find that the small cell, man–made sponges give the best look. Natural sea sponges have extra–large cells and aren't suitable for applying camouflage paint.

Brush Painting

Standard camouflaging can also be applied with a brush. You should have a color picture of the prototype in front of you while you paint, using the illustration as a color guide and for

Figure 5–8

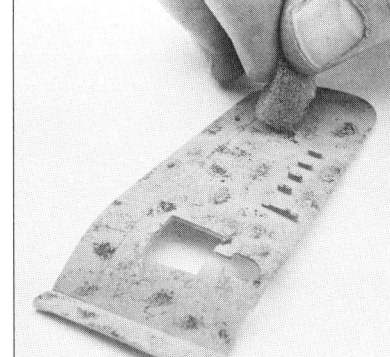

Figure 5–9

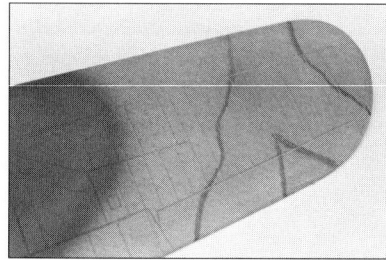

Figure 5–10

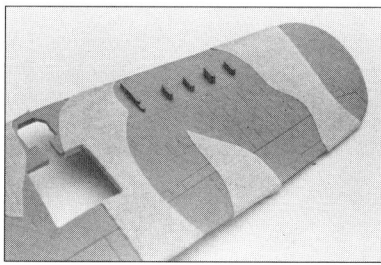

suggestions on how to apply the camouflaging. Of course, no two camouflaged tanks, airplanes, or other vehicles are ever the same in real life, so your model doesn't have to be an exact duplicate. But you should note that some camouflage schemes use only a few colors in large areas, whereas other schemes use as many as five or six colors in small patches.

Apply the lightest color first. This acts as your background. You can paint the entire model (excluding the landing gear, wheels, and other "detail" parts) with this base color. Let it dry. With a pencil (see Figure 5–9), outline the area that you want to paint with the next darkest color. If you make a mistake, rub off the pencil mark. Don't erase it, or you'll end up with a shiny spot. With a 1/4–inch brush, apply the second color, brushing over the pencil marks. Let that color dry; then repeat the process for the remaining colors.

Masking

Some camouflage schemes are complex and freehand brush painting may not yield the best results. To get a fine separation between the colors, use masking tape to mark off the area for the additional colors.

As before, paint the light background color first. Lay some strips of masking tape on a glass or plastic surface (a window will do in a pinch), and use your hobby knife to cut smooth and even curves. Apply the tape on the model as illustrated in Figure 5–10. If the tape is really sticky, touch it to your fingers a few times; the oil of your skin will reduce the stickiness, so there will be less chance that when the tape is removed, it will pull off paint with it.

If the area to be painted is large, use a spray can. Otherwise, add the second color with a paint brush. Paint by starting over the masking tape and brushing toward the surface of the model.

That way, you won't push paint under the masking tape. Wait for the second color to dry completely; then carefully peel off the tape. Repeat the process for each additional color.

Using Stencils

Many attack aircraft of World War II and the Korean War used a unique soft–edge camouflage paint scheme. This can be duplicated by using stencils and spray paint. Advanced model builders often use an airbrush instead of a spray can to apply the paint, but mastering an air brush is an art in itself. Once you get good at basic model building, you can try your hand at air brushing. There are many good books on air brush technique at bookstores and your local library.

You can use any stiff paper for the stencil. You can tape together a bunch of 3– by 5–inch index cards, or use the page dividers provided in most school notebooks. Place the paper on a piece of artboard and cut out small, irregular shapes with your hobby knife (see Figure 5–11). Don't cut out a shape larger than about 3/4 inch, preferably even smaller. Two or three shapes on the entire sheet are enough; you'll obtain various camouflage effects by holding the paper at a different angle to and distance from the model while spraying.

Cover the parts of your model that you don't want sprayed. These include the cockpit or canopy, landing gear, engine, and so forth. Use masking tape or simply cover up the area with paper and tape it in place. Take the model outside and spray the paint through the stencil and onto the model.

Keep these points in mind:

- The further away you hold the stencil to the model, the larger the spot of paint, and the softer (also called "feathered") the edge of the spot will be (see Figure 5–12).
- The closer you hold the stencil to the model, the smaller the spot of paint, and the harder the edge of the spot will be.

Figure 5–11

Figure 5–12

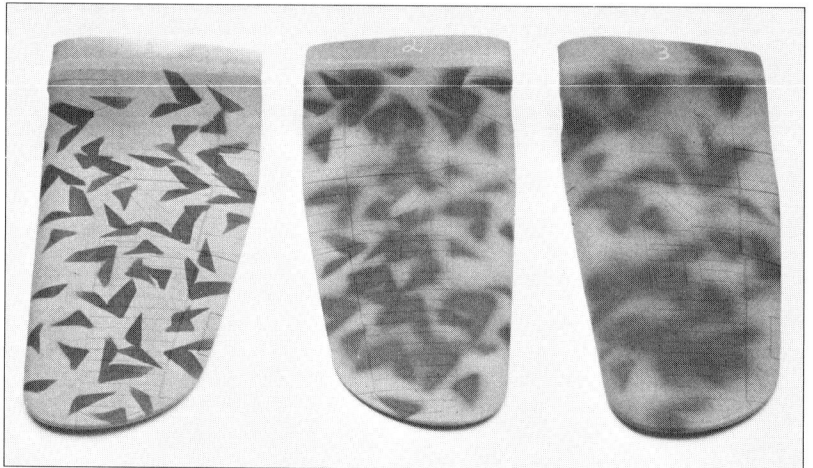

Generally, you will want to place the the stencil about one or two inches from the model. Hold the can of paint six or eight inches from the stencil and spray. Try not to get paint on your fingers or let the paint overspray the paper and splatter on the model. For each new spot, turn the paper slightly or hold it further away from or closer to the model. You can also use one of the other stencils you have cut in the paper. Do a little bit at a time and inspect your work as you go.

SIMPLE WEATHERING TECHNIQUES

From the day they are put in service, military and commercial vehicles and aircraft are subjected to the torments of weathering and age. This is particularly true of tanks and troop vehicles, which get coated with mud, grime, and dirt as they cover vast expanses of territory. Weathering and age come in many forms, and some types are more prominent on certain types of vehicles:

- Everything shows wear from use. You can suggest the amount of use by the wear you give the model. Wear can be characterized by broken parts, worn tires (as described for the F4U kit above), and hasty repairs.
- Chips in the paint are a type of wear common to aircraft. The propeller blades, engine cowling, and leading tips of wings are subjected to the onslaught of debris, which can chip off the paint.
- Soot is from exhaust fumes. Airplanes have a certain

amount of soot trailing from the exhaust pipes; ships have soot coming from the boiler smokestacks. Diesel fuel puts out much more soot than gasoline, so models of diesel–driven prototypes (such as big trucks and non-nuclear ships) show more signs of soot.

- All ships show signs of rust. Even the best–kept naval aircraft carrier has rust somewhere, usually where cables or anchors attach to the hull, on masts, or around portholes. Rust often oozes from small orifices in the ship, so the rust marks look like spilled liquid.
- Hurried maintenance during wartime causes fuel spills. The area around the gas tanks in trucks and airplanes is slightly discolored and shinier than the rest of the vehicle or craft. This is caused by spilled petrol. Fuel spills on diesel–operated vehicles are characterized by a honey shade of brown.
- Likewise during wartime, hasty repairs show signs that replacement parts were used from another airplane or vehicle. This is particularly true of aircraft, where the engine cowling may be from one airplane, the left underwing panels from another, and the rudder from yet another. Of course, the plane wasn't repainted after these quick–fixes, so these items show a different color scheme. You decide whether the color is off a small amount or a great deal.

Signs of Wear

Concentrate on those parts of the model that are subjected to the greatest amount of wear. The tires of the airplane are a good example. The pilot's seat in the cockpit is another place to add the effects of wear. The seats of the F4U, for example, were made of leather, and the combination of constant use and the sea air acted to wear down the seats after just a few months of service. Even though the war ended a few years after the F4U started service in the Pacific, it's likely that the seats in some planes were eventually reduced to just a thin layer of cowhide.

You can approximate the appearance of a worn seat by first painting the seat a neutral "leather" color. Testor brown is a good choice. For the worn part, mix equal measures of brown and gray. Use a technique called "dry brushing" to apply this mixture to the parts of the seat you want to look worn.

With dry brushing, you dip the brush in the paint and then wipe off most of the paint on the sides of the mixing dish or on a piece of paper. With a dab of wet paint still on the brush, you almost rub the paint onto the model.

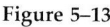
Figure 5–13

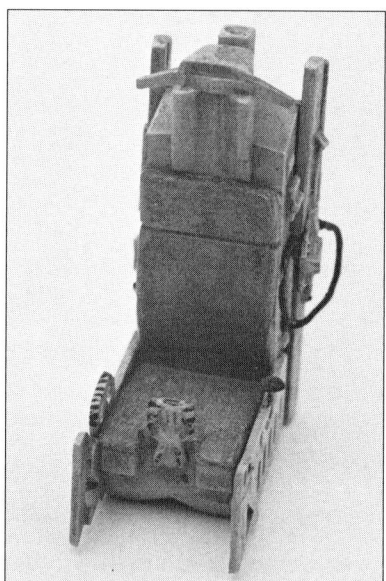

Start from the center of the seat and work up and down and to the sides. Think about how a person sits in a chair. Put the heaviest concentration of paint on the bottom of the seat and at the lower back. There will be little wear on the sides of the side and the top back portion. See Figure 5–13 for an example.

When you gain a little more experience building models, you can break some "non-essential" parts to show the effects of wear. For example, on the F4U you can break off some of the engine cowling petals or perhaps one of the exhaust pipes that stick under the cowling. With a plastic model, you should break parts by sawing or cutting them off. A small razor saw does the trick the best, because you can better control the amount of breakage. You may

cut off too much when using a hobby knife.

Chipped Paint

An airplane that takes off from and lands at makeshift dirt and asphalt runways and travels through the air at a maximum of 425 miles per hour is bound to hit something every once in a while. The effects of collisions with small rocks, pieces of other planes, even sleet and hail, show up as chips and flaked–off paint. On an airplane, the most chips are seen around the propellers and the leading edges of the wings, the rear stabilizer, and the rudder.

You can duplicate these chips by painting small flecks of gray paint on the propeller and wings. Avoid using white or silver paint; unless you do the job just right, the effect will be too

Figure 5–14

chips will be on the left–hand side of the propeller blades. Note that this is the "thick" or leading side of the blade. Figure 5–14 shows the F4U with chip marks at critical locations on the wings and propeller.

Soot

Soot is caused by exhaust fumes from the engine and also the explosive powder of guns, shown in and around the muzzle (barrel) of the armaments. In the F4U, as with all airplanes, the soot is pushed back, deflected by the stream of air as the craft is in flight. You can duplicate soot by mixing a small amount of talcum with black paint (a smaller amount than you used for painting the tires).

The best soot effects are achieved by airbrushing, but you can approximate the look

bright. You want to duplicate the look of the bare metal underneath the paint.

Remember that on an airplane in flight, the majority of the wind goes under the wings (that's what makes the plane go in the air). It stands to reason then that the greatest amount of chipping will be on the underside of the wings. Also remember that in almost all planes, the propeller turns counterclockwise (as you are facing the craft), so that most all of the with dry brushing. Get as much paint off the brush as you can and, starting from the exhaust pipes, brush towards the rear of the plane, as shown in Figure 5–15. Paint in and around the pipes for good measure, too. For the greatest realism, the outside of the pipes should be painted dark brown or rust. This is the color that almost all exhaust pipes—even in cars—take on after a short period of use.

The soot from the black powder of the six machine guns of the F4U (three guns in each of the wings) can be seen around the leading edge of the wing. The soot trail on the wings is very small, averaging no more than just a few inches on a real F4U. You can duplicate the look by dabbing the black paint/talcum powder mixture around the opening of the guns and smearing just a little bit on the wings.

Rust

Rust is typical on any metal object (other than ones made out of aluminum or copper) that's exposed to moist air or water. The F4U flew over the water for almost all of its missions, and the moist sea air certainly contributed to rust. You can dab rust–colored paint on a number of points on the model, such as around the canopy, near the landing gear, and around the gray chips you painted on to

Figure 5–15

Figure 5–16

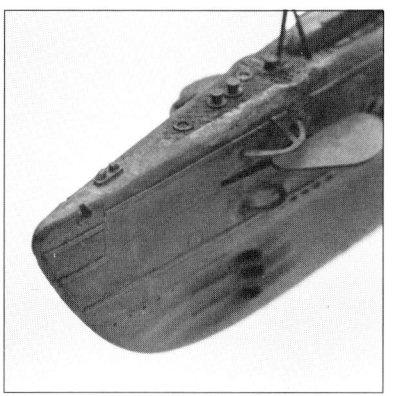

depict impact with small objects during flight.

Rust is much more common on ships and submarines. With these, the rust oozes out of portholes and other openings, and looks as if someone spilled coffee over the side of the ship. Getting this effect isn't always easy, however, and it takes some practice. The best method is to dry brush rust–colored paint in a teardrop shape. As

illustrated in Figure 5–16, use more paint for the top of the rust mark than the bottom.

Incidentally, don't make the rust mark too big, especially on a 1/72–scale aircraft carrier model. Just a small dab of rust on and around the anchor and the bottom of the portholes, around the propeller and rudder, and other likely places should be enough.

Fuel Spills

Gasoline spills can be duplicated by applying Glosscote to the surface of the model. Use a brush to build up several coats in an inverted teardrop shape. If the entire model is sprayed with Dullcote as a protective cover, paint the fuel spill afterward. If you get good at mixing paints, you can mix a small amount of black or gray with the back-

ground color and apply it to simulate a fuel spill.

Diesel fuel spills have a transparent brown look to them, which is difficult to duplicate with paint. A suitable mixture for simulating diesel fuel spills can be obtained by adding Dullcote to brown paint. Add more Dullcote than brown paint to make the concoction semi–transparent. Although Dullcote is a lacquer and model paint is an enamel, and the two really shouldn't be mixed, it's acceptable in this instance because the result is supposed to look like a mottled, oozing mess. A lighter mixture can be used to simulate a heavy concentration of gasoline spills.

Chipped Decals

The more aging you give your models, the more you will have

to chip the decals to match. Before you chip away at any decal, however, practice on a discarded decal and model part to get the technique right. Don't experiment with a model you have spent hours perfecting.

The easiest way to chip a decal is to work on it while it's still in its wet and weak form. Before the decal has time to set up, break off a portion with a hobby knife, pencil eraser, or other instrument. When the decal is wet, it will break rather easily, so go slowly. Take out a small

portion at a time. The end result should look like the picture in Figure 5–17.

You can also chip away at the decal after it has dried. Carefully scrape it off using the adzing technique described in Chapter 3. Once the decal has been scraped to your liking, you may want to paint chips onto the surface, as you did with the propellers and wings. Apply the paint carefully, using a number 0 (or smaller) brush over the area where you have removed the decal.

Protective Overcoats

You should protect the detailing of your models by spraying on a thin coat of Dullcote or Glosscote. Almost all military vehicles, airplanes, and ships should be oversprayed with Dullcote to give them a uniform

flat finish. In any case, you will need to spray Dullcote or Glosscote if you are going to apply decals to the model. Remember that decals do not adhere well to flat finish paints. To protect the decals, apply another thin coat of Dullcote when you are through.

How to Mix Paints

Mixing paints to achieve a unique color is a science, and it will take many attempts before you get consistent results. Don't expect to mix paints like the pros on your first try. It takes patience and an understanding of color theory.

There are three primary colors of paints: red, blue, and yellow. You obtain all other colors by mixing these three together. A second set of three colors, called secondary colors, is created by

Figure 5–17

mixing equal amounts of the primary colors. The three secondary colors are purple (sometimes called violet), orange, and green. The secondary colors help in advanced color mixing, since they are themselves mixed colors.

The color wheel in Figure 5–18 shows the relationship of the primary and secondary colors. Colors opposite one another are contrasting or complementary colors, so called because they are—in terms of color—as far apart from one another as they can possibly be. You can see that the complement of purple is yellow, because purple is made with red and blue, and has no yellow in it.

If you are familiar with the visible light spectrum, you know that the collection of six colors are the ones you see when sunlight is broken into its colors by a prism. The spectrum starts at red and goes around the wheel to purple.

When you mix colors, you will most often use primary or secondary colors. The results are the most predictable. As you gain experience in mixing colors, you can try combining primary and secondary colors to make elaborate compound colors, like tan, gold, silver, and purple. A color wheel (as in Figure 5–18) can show you what kind of results you can expect.

Figure 5–18

When mixing paint, always start with small amounts. Don't mix the contents of two or more bottles together and hope for the best. Use an eyedropper so you can carefully meter the amount of paint you are mixing. Write down the number of drops of paint you use of each color and keep your notes in a notebook for future reference.

Pour a bit of the lightest color paint into a bowl and add a few drops of the darker paint. Stir with a wooden ice cream stick or toothpick. Do one or two drops at a time. If you mix in too many drops at once, you may make the mixture too dark. Lightening the color of paint is difficult, even for the pros.

You should mix only as much paint as you will need, but you should never mix less. Even with an eyedropper, the amount of each color in your custom–mixed paints will vary from batch to batch. If you have to make more of a color to complete a paint job, it will invariably be darker or lighter than the first mixture.

If you make too much paint, you can store it for later use in a paint bottle that's been thoroughly flushed out. Keep the cap on tight and it should last for many months. To help you remember what the paint looks like, dab a little bit of it on a scrap piece of plastic. Let the scrap dry, label it with the name or formulation of your custom color, and keep it handy for future reference.

About the F4U-1D Corsair

Invariably, building a model gets you interested in the real thing. If you are earnest about model building, you will scour books in the library to learn as much about the prototype as you possibly can. Here is some information obtained about the F4U Corsair aircraft from several military aircraft source-books. They tell about the design, history, and use of this amazing airplane. Knowing these details will enhance your appreciation of the real F4U as well as help you add authentic detail to your model.

The F4U–1D was originally designed by Tex B. Beisel, the head designer of aircraft manufacturing giant Vought. The project was started in 1938, following a request by the U.S. Navy for an agile and fast aircraft that could be used in carrier operations. The original design, the XF4U–1 (the "X" stands for "experimental"), used the powerful Pratt & Whitney XR–2800 Double Wasp

18–cylinder radial engine, which developed 2,000 horsepower. The engine was just being perfected at the time of the design of the F4U, which employed a compact airframe with an unusual "gull wing" design.

The maiden flight of the XF4U "Corsair" was on May 29, 1940, and although it set the record for the first U.S. fighter to exceed an airspeed of 400 miles per hour (it was actually clocked at 404 mph), it had many problems. The most critical was its relatively poor fire power. To strengthen the fire power, the fuel tanks had to be repositioned, which also meant relocating the cockpit almost three feet to the rear. With the original canopy design, this made forward visibility, especially of the ground below, extremely poor. The plane was therefore judged unsuitable for carrier missions—the exact reason for its original design!

Production of the F4U began in June 1941, six months before the bombing of Pearl Harbor and the official entry of the U.S. in World War II. (Europe had been at war since September 1, 1939, when Germany invaded Poland.)

By the end of 1942, the Navy took possession of 178 aircraft, but waited until April 1944, when a new and improved version came out, before committing to buy more of them—and to use them on carriers.

In the meantime, the F4U saw combat with land–based Marine Corps squadrons, as depicted in the 1976–78 television series "Baa Baa Black Sheep," starring Robert Conrad. The F4U helped prove itself in February 1943, at Guadalcanal, as well as many on other missions thereafter.

The F4U–1D, an improved version that came out in 1944, encompassed many design refinements, including a re–engineered canopy for better pilot's vision and a more powerful engine. The F4U–1D was the most popular of the Corsair series and was manufactured in the greatest number: 4,102 by Vought, 3,808 by Goodyear (who called them the FG–1); and 725 by Brewster (who called them the F3A–1). The F4U–1D was manufactured up until 1947, two years after the end of World War II; they were replaced by similar aircraft with a more powerful engine and armaments.

The F4U–1D Corsair proved to be an important factor in assuring success in the Pacific for the U.S. In a total of 64,051 missions, the F4U shot down 2,140 enemy aircraft. Yet in all those missions, only 189 F4U's were lost. That's a ratio of over 11 to 1, great odds even for today's ace "Top Gun" pilots!

Here are the nuts–and–bolts specifications for the Vought F4U–1D Corsair:

Engine: Pratt & Whitney R–2800–8W Double Wasp—18 cylinder, radial, air–cooled, 2,000 horsepower thrust
Wingspan: 41 feet
Length: 33 feet, 4 1/2 inches
Height: 15 feet, 1 inch
Weight: 14,000 pounds (loaded, fueled)
Maximum level flight speed: 425 miles per hour (at 20,000 feet altitude)
Service ceiling: 37,000 feet
Range: 1,015 miles
Armament: 6 machine guns; 2,000 pounds of bombs
Crew: 1

Chapter 6

Building
Action
Models

Action promotes realism. With a sense of action, models seem to come alive, as if you could actually drive, fly, or pilot the thing. If only you were smaller, you think, you could jump right in that Sikorsky Black Hawk attack helicopter and cruise over the countryside.

Action shows a model in a way similar to the way the prototype might look in real life. The action may be conveyed by the addition of a human figure riding in a jeep, an airplane canopy in the open–and–ready position, a broken–down tank, or a crew loading bombs under the wings of an F8F–2 "Bearcat." You add the sense of action as you build and finish the model, providing the details with paint, decals, and other techniques as you have learned in previous chapters.

In this chapter, you'll learn how to apply some of your new experience in creating models that—in a sense—have a life of their own. You can use just one of these techniques or combine them all, as you see fit. Some action is best described in a realistic setting. Information about how to produce action settings and other displays is in Chapter 7.

TECHNIQUES FOR CARS

When you think of cars, you think of them, not standing still on some featureless display stand, but screaming down the road. This is particularly true if you are building sports cars, like the Testor Porsche 911 or Lamborghini Silhouette. Cars are meant to be driven, and there are a variety of techniques you can use to convey motion or use.

Turn the Wheels

If the model permits it, turn the front wheels as if the car itself is in a turn. Not all model kits allow this without modification to the front axle or body parts.

Open the Hood and Trunk

No one drives with the hood or trunk open, but it shows that the model is more than a plastic shell with wheels. Most model kits are designed so that you can open the hood and trunk at will, so be sure you don't cement it closed.

If the model comes with engine parts, carefully construct it and mount it in the engine compartment. If you have done a good job, show off your handiwork and keep the lid open, as shown in Figure 6–1. Or you can open the trunk. Use a piece of

Figure 6–1

charcoal–colored felt (or use gray felt lightly painted with black) as the "carpet" that lines the inside of the trunk.

Add Action Figures

Cars are mostly done in 1/24 scale, which is a standard size for human action figures. If the car kit comes with a driver, consider painting the figure and placing him or her in the driver's seat.

Even if the kit doesn't come with figures, you can purchase them separately at most hobby stores. They are available in a variety of poses and "costumes." The figures don't come painted; that's up to you. We'll show you how to paint action figures later in this chapter.

Some examples: You could add an action figure of someone leaning over and looking into the engine compartment, perhaps trying to fix something. Or how about showing the figure changing the tire (add a figure to Figure 6–2)? Salvage a similar size tire from another model and use it as a "spare," which you can display propped up against your model. Use the technique covered in Chapter 5 to flatten plastic and rubber tires. Flatten it excessively to show a "blow out."

Don't Forget Detail

Small, not-so-obvious details can also provide a sense of

Figure 6–2

Italian, and Rolls Royces are English. Many cars in Europe are driven through other European countries, and have a separate plate for each one. Add the additional plates near the trunk and bumper.

For far–out effects, break a headlight or tailight, or add rust or mud to the bottom edge of the car chassis. Thick mud can be created by mixing flour and white glue. Apply it with a toothpick to the bottom of the car as illustrated in Figure 6–3. When the mixture is dry, paint it dark brown. (Be sure to use Dullcote or Glosscote spray on the entire model; the coating will help protect the mud detail.)

Avoid overdoing the unusual effects. Too much detail can make a model look unrealistic. Only when you are an experienced model maker should you attempt

action. Unless you want the car to be "showroom perfect," add soot at the exhaust. Lighten the tires to show wear. Mar the paint lightly along the sides to show the effect of doors from other cars chipping at the finish.

If the kit doesn't come with a license plate decal, purchase a few at the hobby store. Pick your favorite state and apply the license plates to the front and rear of the car. If the automobile is European, and you want to make it appear as if the car is driven in Europe, use one of the European plates that are available. Some guidelines: Porsches are German, Lamborghinis are such effects as bashed fenders and other serious accidents.

TECHNIQUES FOR MILITARY VEHICLES

Military vehicles offer the greatest chance for adding in–action detail. Military vehicles include Jeeps, troop transports, tanks, armored cars, half–tracks, guns–on–trailers, and more.

When building a military vehicle model, you have three general choices, as depicted in Figure 6–4:

- Make it look brand- new, ready for the general's inspection.

- Make it look as if it's currently in combat.
- Make it look as if it's through with combat, and now is home in the junk yard or museum.

Making the model look new is an easy job: just paint the pieces as usual and add a little "wear and tear" detail. But since most of us are used to seeing military vehicles in action, or the physical effects of action on tanks and other vehicles, this approach does little to convey realism.

A tank that's seen all the combat it can take may have broken tank treads, or it may be missing critical components, such as its cannon and guns. It may have parts fully rusted or torn off. Duplicating this type of condition can be difficult, so it's best to wait until you gain more experience.

Figure 6–3

Figure 6–4

Tanks in combat may appear only slightly damaged or almost completely inoperative. A condition midway between these two is a good balance. The model looks real, but the technique for adding action detail is not terribly difficult.

Tank Tracks

Tank tracks receive a lot of beating during their use. You should paint on specks of rust all around the track area, including the road wheels. Add mud using the mud mixture described in the previous section. To look authentic, the track should sag around the idler wheels. The track material provided with most tank kits is flexible vinyl, which has a natural "bounce" to it. For best results, you must form the tread to produce the sagging effect.

After installing the tread, the easiest way to add sag is to use black thread and tie or glue the thread to the inside of the tread (see Figure 6–5). Then wrap it around the axle of the nearest road wheel below. If the thread is attached properly, as close to the body of the track as possible, it should not be very noticeable.

Sometimes the thread can't be concealed, in which case you need to add small pins or blocks to keep the tracks pressed down. The pins or blocks can be discarded plastic from extra parts or runners, glued to the side of the tank and painted to match the rest of the vehicle. To set the pins, use a small drill to make a hole and insert the pins into the hole, as shown in Figure 6– 6. Use cement to keep the pins in place. You can use a pin vise for drilling or a small hand drill. Be sure that the hole is the

92

Figure 6–5

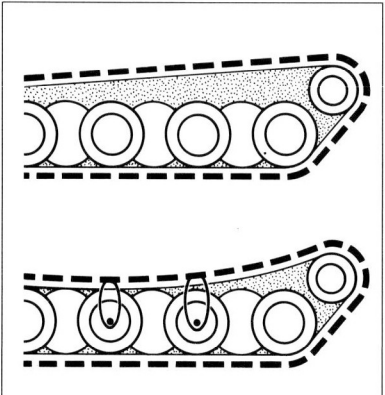

Figure 6–6

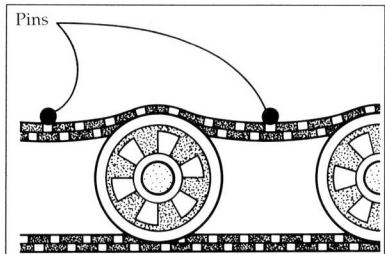

Pins shown oversize for clarity

same size as the pin you are using, or the pin will fall out before the cement has time to dry.

Camouflage Painting

Military vehicles are almost always painted camouflage. The color scheme depends on the theater of operations (desert camouflage is greatly different from jungle camouflage), the time period, the vehicle's country of origin, and the branch of service. The camouflage is typically applied to the entire vehicle, including truck bed covers and sometimes even the rims of wheels. You should duplicate this with your camouflage paint job.

Use whatever painting method is best for you: brush or stencil spray. The pros use an airbrush to apply camouflage paint colors. Most hobby stores have inexpensive air brush kits that you can try. Practice mixing and thinning paint, and then applying it to white cardboard before you try camouflaging your model.

Weathering and Detail

Military vehicles receive the harshest punishment, so don't be afraid to go heavy on the weather effects. Many military vehicles run on diesel fuel (particularly tanks) so add lots of diesel soot around the exhaust pipe. Figure 6–7 shows typical weathering for a tank; you can apply similar techniques to other types of military vehicles, as well.

The guns and cannons in many military vehicle kits, especially tanks and armored cars, are made of solid molded plastic. What gun or cannon doesn't have a hole in the barrel? You can provide the hole by carefully drilling out the business end of the gun or cannon. For small caliber guns, use the tip of a hobby knife or hat pin. For larger guns and cannons, use a pin vice and miniature drills. The hole doesn't need to be more than 1/4 inch deep. If you make a mistake and drill the hole off center or through the barrel, you can readily fix it by filling the hole with putty, sanding it down, and starting again.

If the outside of the guns and cannon is painted in camouflage (which they usually are), paint the inside of the barrel gun metal black or flat black. Use a small–tipped brush, such as a 00 or 000, dip it in the paint bottle, and then wipe off as much paint as possible. (Otherwise excess paint settles in the barrel and takes forever to dry.) Stick the brush tip into the barrel. Wipe off any excess around the outside of the barrel.

If you later paint the outside of the barrel (especially with spray paint), stuff the end of the barrel with a piece of damp cloth or cotton that will prevent you from overpainting inside the barrel.

Adding Action Figures

Military vehicles are always driven by somebody, so don't neglect adding people to your models. See the section below on how to paint realistic human action figures. If the model kit doesn't come with action figures, buy a selection at a hobby store.

Provide more than just the driver. Most armored cars,

Figure 6–7

Figure 6–8

TECHNIQUES FOR AIRCRAFT

Adding the illusion of action to aircraft can be tough, particularly if you choose, as most modelers do, to display the plane on the ground. The alternative is to display the aircraft from the ceiling by a wire. If the plane has retractable landing gear, you can display the model with the landing gear up.

Ready–to–Go Airplane

The best way to convey action with an airplane is to show it ready for a mission. If the craft has underwing bombs, attach one bomb and leave the other on the ground, as if it is about to be mounted. Place the ground crew around the plane, perhaps ready to hoist the bomb and attach it to the wing.

transports, and tanks have several people on board. When adding action figures to tanks, open the commander's hatch or escape hatch to show the people inside. Your figures should all have different poses, as shown in Figure 6–8.

One favorite action figure is of a soldier peering through a pair of binoculars. That's a perfect figure for the commander of a tank, as he stands in the hatch on the top of the turret.

Figure 6–9

Show the pilot in the cockpit or just climbing into the cockpit. If possible, keep the canopy open, to show the pilot and interior of the cockpit.

Weathering

You can suggest heavy action with weathering. Apply the weathering techniques you learned in the previous chapter. Figure 6–9 gives you some ideas on how to weather a typical World War II era airplane.

PAINTING ACTION FIGURES

The best way to convey action is to put people in with your models. Many beginning model enthusiasts shy away from using action figures because they look fake when unpainted, yet a good paint job is extremely difficult. It's true that good action figure painting requires a great deal of expertise and patience. But a few practical tips can get you on your way to creating amazingly realistic action figures.

Painting the Face

The pros carefully mix paints to create faces with many colors and textures. If you look at a good painting, you'll note that the face is not a solid layer of flesh–colored paint. Practically the entire spectrum of color is seen in a person's face, and the artist's eye brings out those colors to create a realistic look.

Until you become skillful at painting action figures, you can stick with using flesh tone for the face and other exposed body parts. With a small fine–tipped brush, such as a 000, coat the face, arms, neck, and other areas with oil–based flesh paint. The paint is available at art supply stores and comes in various sizes of tubes. A small tube will last you a long time.

Let the paint dry. Paint the clothes the appropriate color. (You can use ordinary model enamels for the clothes.) If the figure is dressed in battle fatigues, use a drab olive green. Boots can either be black or light and dark green. If you are unsure of the color scheme, look at a soldier's garb in a magazine or book.

Figure 6–10

Now go back and provide the details. (Be sure the previous coat of paint has dried completely.) Use tan paint (or a mixture of brown and white) for the eyes and teeth. Don't use white; it's too bright and looks unreal-istic. After the light color in the eyes has dried, cover most of it (except, say, the bottom and sides), with dark brown or dark tan. Don't leave the eyes un-filled, or your action figures will look as if they have just seen a ghost! The results of painting action figures are shown in Figure 6–10.

When you are satisfied with the look of the basic figure, you can let it dry and then add a protective coat of Dullcote. Position the figure in or next to your model. If you want it to be a permanent part of your model, cement or glue it in place.

Chapter 7

Displaying
Your
Models

After you have put in so many hours building your model, you should do more than just stuff it into a bedroom drawer. Display it, so you can periodically gaze at your creation and remember the good time you had building it. While your model is on display, others can view your hard work as well, and they can appreciate the care and detail that went into it.

There are many types of displays, from simple to sophisticated. Here in this chapter, we'll show you how to display your models on wood and plastic bases, how to create interesting and unique backgrounds with easy–to–find art materials, and more.

WOOD AND PLASTIC STANDS

Many of your models can be displayed, by themselves with no stand, on top of your dresser or on a shelf. Position them to your liking, but be sure that nothing will fall on them. Periodically dust them off with a feather duster or use a bulb blower, available at camera stores.

Your special models can be mounted on wood and plastic stands. You can handle the model more easily when it is on the stand, and the model is less likely to fall over and break. If you have added action figures and other elements around the model, similar to the action figure shown in Figure 7–1, you'll want to use a stand to keep everything together.

Figure 7–1

Figure 7–2

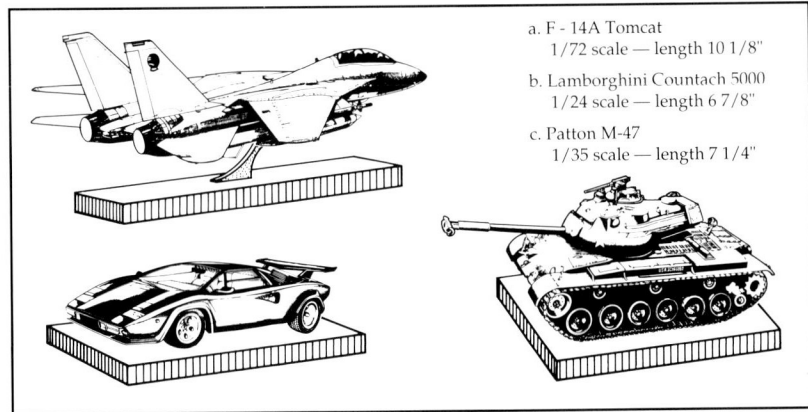

a. F - 14A Tomcat
1/72 scale — length 10 1/8"

b. Lamborghini Countach 5000
1/24 scale — length 6 7/8"

c. Patton M-47
1/35 scale — length 7 1/4"

Wood Stands

You can use any piece of wood for your stand, but a solid wood (as opposed to plywood or particle board) is better. One source of inexpensive pieces of wood is cabinet shops. Ask if you can buy a couple of pieces from the scrap pile. Plaques at trophy supply stores are another good source for wood for stands. The trophy plaques are usually high–quality hardwoods, like oak, walnut, and mahogany.

The piece should be about the same size as the model or perhaps a little larger. If you are displaying an airplane, you can make the stand long and thin. Mount the plane lengthwise on the stand. Dimensions for some common models are shown in Figure 7–2. Cut the wood to the desired size with a hand saw, or if you know how, with a power saw. Be certain you observe all safety precautions when handling woodworking tools, or you may be hurt.

After cutting, smooth the surfaces and edges of the stand. Use a medium–grit sandpaper and work the wood until it is as smooth as possible. Remove the wood dust with a tac cloth (available at hardware stores). Stain the wood if you want it darker. Wipe–on stain is the easiest to use and dries quickly. Whether or not you apply stain, you should brush or spray on a protective coat. You can use Testor Dullcote for a satin luster finish or Glosscote for a shiny, glossy finish.

Permanently attach the model, if you wish, to the stand with white glue, or better yet, with 5–minute epoxy. Mix the epoxy as recommended; then dab a little on the bottom of the model. If mounting an airplane model, dab small amounts of epoxy or glue under the wheels. If you apply too much, and the epoxy or glue oozes out from under the wheels, wipe it up quickly. Even after the adhesive is set, the model will come off the base if you handle it roughly.

Plastic Stands

Non–military models can often be displayed on a plastic stand. The plastic helps to accentuate the colors and finish of the model, particularly if the model is a "showroom" new race car. If the plastic is clear, it tends to disappear into the background, and you see only the model.

Plastic is available at plastic specialty stores and plastic fabricators (look in the Yellow Pages under "Plastic"). You can buy plastic sheets in a variety of sizes and colors. Most stores have a scrap pile that may have the exact piece you are looking for. The price for most small scrap pieces, suitable for use as model stands, is under $2.

For the ultimate in plastic stands, get a large acrylic block—something on the order of one or two inches thick. Get the people at the plastic store or fabricator to cut the block to size and burnish (smooth) the edges. The block is now ready for use as a stand.

Working with plastic is only slightly harder than working with wood. Plastic can crack and break, so always use sharp, fine–tooth saws. A hacksaw or coping saw with a metal working blade can be used on acrylic plastic sheet. Work slowly. After you have cut the stand to size, use fine–grit wet/dry sandpaper to smooth the edges. You can use the paper wet or dry.

After the plastic piece has been cut to size and sanded, you can mount the model on it. Use white glue or 5-minute epoxy, as you did with the wood stand. Don't use model cement to glue the model to the plastic. Modeling cement will not work with acrylic plastic.

If the plastic is not already colored, you can paint it any color you desire. Testor spray paints cover acrylic plastic in one coat. By spraying on the underside of the plastic piece (the side opposite the model), you will get a brilliant, glossy look on the top side, even if you use a flat finish paint. Spraying on the top yields the finish of the paint you are using (see Figure 7–3). Use stick–on rubber pads, available at hardware stores, to lift the base off ground level.

SCALE BACKGROUND STANDS AND BASES

With a little bit of ingenuity, you can make a scale background stand or base, which looks like real ground. The effect is ideal for things like model airplanes and helicopters. With just a few

cans and bottles of paint, you can make the base look like a piece of runway.

Use a piece of artboard or cardboard as the base for your model (you can also use wood). Plain white, untextured artboard is perfect for the job. Get a piece a little larger than the model. The base can be cut square or any shape you like. Don't make it

too large, or you'll have trouble finding a spot for it in your room!

Let's assume you are painting a runway for your F–18 fighter jet. You want the markings on the runway to be in scale, so you have to do a little bit of computing. Testor F–18 Hornet is 1/72 scale, so every inch on the model represents 72 inches on the real prototype. Many runways are made of concrete that has been poured in 15– or 20–foot squares. You can see the joining lines in the concrete if you look at the runway from overhead.

Assume that each square is 20 feet by 20 feet. At 1/72 scale, the squares should be 3.3 by 3.3 inches. Here is how we came up with these figures: Take the size of the real–life prototype, and if it is in feet, multiply by 12 to get inches. Divide the number of inches by 72. Twenty feet times

Figure 7–3

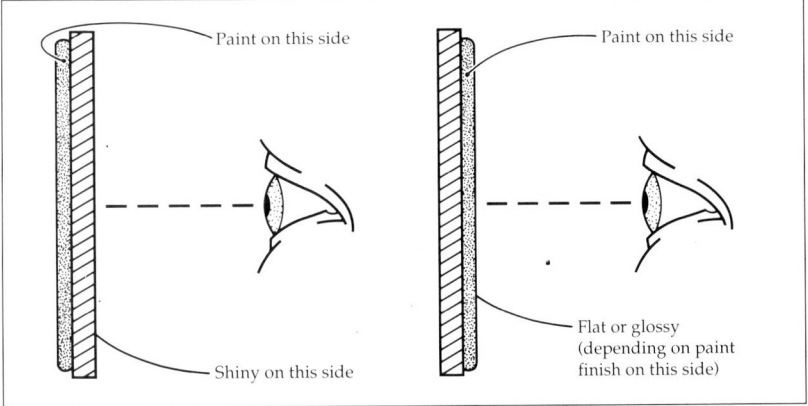

12 is 240 inches; 240 inches divided by 72 is 3.33 inches.

But before you draw the lines for the squares, prepare the runway so it looks like concrete. You can simulate concrete color with light gray paint (you may want to mix some tan in there, too). Spray the entire piece of artboard and let it dry. If you look at concrete—whether it is on a road, building, or runway—you'll notice that it has many shades. Use the dry brush technique with the special mixture of gray paint mixed with a little brown. Use this mixture to make the dark areas.

The darkness is pronounced around the joining lines between each concrete square. With a pencil, mark the squares about 3 3/8 inches apart. Use a ruler or other straight edge to insure a straight line. Go over the lines with the mixed gray/brown paint. After the paint is dry, use your pencil to draw the concrete lines once again. Go over them with a felt–tip pen.

You can now secure the plane to the artboard. Glue or epoxy may not sufficiently hold the model. For an extra–strong bond, wire the wheels of the plane to the artboard. Here's how: Push a thin piece of black wire through the artboard. Wrap the wire around the wheels of the plane, then push

Figure 7–4

the wire against the wheels to help hide it. If the wire shows too much, try it again.

You can also mount action figures and other models to the base, as long as they are to scale. For example, you could add a 1/72–scale fuel truck along with a few 1/72–scale action figures for a pilot and ground crew. Figure 7–4 shows the runway base, the plane, and a few assorted action figures.

Figure 7–5

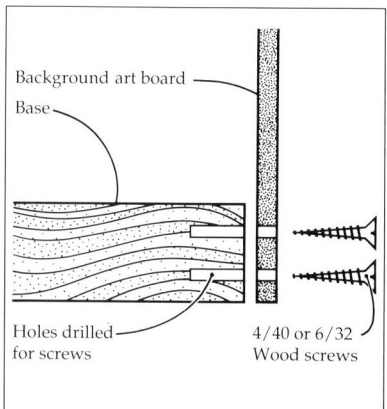

COLOR BACKGROUNDS

Another way to add realism to your displayed models is to use a colored background. You can use the background by itself and mount the model on a wood or plastic stand, or you can combine the background with the artboard base discussed in the last section.

Background Materials

Photograph blowups and posters make good background material. Photographs enlarged to 8 by 10 inches or 11 by 14 inches are ideal with 1/72–scale models. When enlarging a slide or negative, be sure that the original photo is sharp and clear.

If you are taking the picture for the background, be sure to hold the camera steady and focus the lens properly. Use a slow ISO

film (under 200 ISO) to minimize the grainy appearance of faster films. A good rule of thumb is that if the picture looks fuzzy or grainy in the regular 3- by 5–inch size, it will look much worse when blown up. Most neighborhood photo finishing stores will enlarge color slides and negatives for you. The cost is usually under $5 to $7.

Mounting the Picture

When you get the photo back from the lab, mount it on a piece of artboard. You can use contact cement or spray-on adhesive. With the photo securely mounted to the artboard, you can use it as the background. Prop the artboard behind the model or stand, or physically attach it to the stand. For best results, drill small holes, and secure the photo artboard to the model base with 4/40 or 6/32 wood screws (see Figure 7–5).

Figure 7–6

create what's known as a diorama. Dioramas are popular with military model enthusiasts. In addition to a tank or artillery model, the diorama includes action figures, guns, cannons, burned-out buildings, and other evidence of a war-torn area.

The most important consideration is that everything in the diorama must be to scale. If you are using parts from other models, be sure those parts are the same scale as the main model. You lose realism when many scales are used in one diorama. Figure 7–7 shows a rather sophisticated diorama. You won't be able to duplicate this with your first try, but it is something to work towards.

PHOTOGRAPHING YOUR MODELS

Want to show your relatives and friends in other towns the

Follow the same procedure when using a poster. The picture on the poster can be as simple as a cloudy sky (good for airplane displays) or it can be a busy city street. The scale of the picture on the poster can be just about anything, as long as it isn't larger than the scale of the model. When the scale is smaller, it just looks as if the background is further away. Figure 7–6 shows a model with a poster background. The poster was cut to size and mounted on a piece of artboard.

Building Dioramas

By putting your model in a setting with a background, you

Figure 7–7

FIgure 7–8

If you want more than a snapshot, use a 35 mm camera with a good lens. The best results are obtained when using a lens with a macro focus feature, or close–up supplementary lenses attached to the regular lens on your camera. A suitable camera setup is shown in Figure 7–8.

Load your camera with film. If you want large prints (over 5 by 7 inches), use a relatively low ISO speed film. A 100 or 200 ISO speed is ideal. The film is sensitive enough for general picture–taking, even in shade, yet the film isn't too grainy when blown up to large print sizes.

Take your model (along with the background, base, stand, or diorama) outside. If the day is overcast, you can place the model out in the open on a table or stand. If you are shooting the

models you have built? You can't easily pack up your models and mail them across country;

your models are far too fragile and they could break. The next best thing: a photograph.

Just about any camera will do if all you need is a snapshot of your model. You can use a 35 mm camera, a disc camera, or a 110 cartridge film camera. Use color print or slide film, or if you like to do your own developing and printing, black and white film.

model alone (with perhaps a wood or plastic base), lay a light–colored covering over the table or other work area. The covering acts as a backdrop for the model and makes the picture look better. You can use fabric, colored art paper, construction paper, or whatever. Be sure that the backdrop is larger than the model.

If the sun is out, find a shaded area. For example, go under a window awning or open the garage door and position yourself under the door. Try to avoid direct sunlight and partial shade. If you are in only partial shade, like under a tree, your picture may not come out right.

Place the camera on a tripod, if you have one. Using a tripod makes photographing your model much easier. Get very close to the model and focus the camera. If you are using a zoom lens with a macro, go to the macro setting for focusing. If you are using supplementary close–up lenses on your regular picture–taking lens, attach the lens and then focus. Move the camera closer to or farther away from the model to get the picture you want. Remember: If it doesn't look focused in the viewfinder, it won't be in focus in the picture.

Most 35 mm cameras have a built–in exposure meter. Use the meter to determine the proper exposure for your model picture. If you are using a tripod, you can use a slow shutter speed—down to about 1/8 or 1/4 of a second. Use a shutter release cable to snap the picture and be sure the camera doesn't move when the shutter is open. If you are holding the camera in your hands as you take the picture, don't use a shutter speed slower than 1/30 of a second. The picture may blur if you use slow shutter speeds.

When taking pictures up close, only a small portion of the scene will be in focus. The so–called "depth of field" will be very narrow, so even though you may focus on one portion of your model, the rest of your model—which is farther away from the camera—may be out of focus. Figure 7–9 shows this.

You can increase the depth of field by adjusting the aperture (or f/stop) of the camera. The larger the f/stop number, the smaller the aperture. With a small aperture, you increase the depth of field (see Figure 7–10), so more of your picture is in focus. Always try an f/stop of f/8 or higher when taking close–up pictures of your models. Adjust the shutter speed as indicated

Figure 7–9

Figure 7–10

by the exposure meter to compensate for the smaller aperture.

You can largely eliminate depth–of–field problems by better positioning of the model and the camera. Avoid shots where the camera is very low and where one part of the model is much closer to the camera than the other parts. When taking a picture of your model plane on a runway base, for example, position the camera high up. Pick a spot in the center of the model to focus on. Try a number of different positions just in case the first picture doesn't come out.

Even though you may be taking the pictures with the help of a built–in exposure meter, some pictures may turn out too light or too dark. Try a shot at the exposure indicated by the meter. Then try two more shots one f/stop or shutter speed setting higher and lower than recommended.

As with model building, getting good at photographing your handiwork takes time and experience, too. Try a roll and see how it turns out. Keep a logbook and write down the settings you made for each picture. Compare your results with the prints or slides you get back.

Chapter 8

How the
Pros
Do It

Making models from plastic kits goes way beyond the techniques presented in this book. With each new model you build, your skills and model–making knowledge will increase. Keep at this exciting hobby and you'll be a pro, with models good enough to show at exhibitions and contests.

This chapter will introduce you to a number of techniques used by the pros, those who consider model building both an art and a science—not to mention a challenge. Use the techniques in the following pages as ideas to stimulate you and to get you thinking like a modeling expert. If you care to learn more about how the pros build models, look in your local library for additional books and periodicals on the subject of plastic model building.

WORKING WITH TREE

The tree, also called the runner, is the plastic piece that holds together all the model parts. The tree is made in the molding process; hot plastic is injected into the mold through small conduits, called gates. At the end of the conduits the plastic enters the mold, which forms the final part of the kit.

Since the tree is the same plastic (even the same color) as the parts, you can use it for your model. The kind of plastic used in model kits becomes soft when heated, and when it is soft you can form it into all sorts of shapes.

The best heat source for working with tree is an ordinary candle. To heat the tree, hold a piece in both hands and swirl it quickly around the tip of the flame, as shown in Figure 8–1. If you get

the plastic too close to the fire, it will turn black and may be ruined. Be sure that the plastic does not actually catch fire. When plastic burns, it gives off a strong odor. If a piece of tree you are working with accidentally catches on fire, douse it in a can of water (keep the water nearby just in case) and air out the room. Avoid breathing the fumes of the burned plastic.

Once the plastic softens, you can gently pull it apart to make fine plastic thread or even bend the tree to make angled pipes or cables. With practice, you'll learn how to work the tree to get just the result you want. Don't expect to get it right the first time around.

One common use for tree includes making the guy wires in older airplanes. You're probably familiar with the guy wires in

Figure 8–1

Figure 8–2

World War I planes that connected the two (sometimes three) wings. Antennae were

used in airplanes during World War II and the Korean War. These wires often stretched from the canopy to the rudder or stabilizer (see Figure 8–2). Another common use for tree is for making cables and tubing, for airplane cockpits and engines, even the umbilical cord for astronauts working outside the Space Shuttle.

Once the tree has cooled, you can cement and paint it just like any other plastic part. Use only a tiny bit of glue or use white glue. If the tree piece is large enough, you can sand and file it to just about any shape.

AIRBRUSHING

Airbrushing is a lot like painting with a spray can, but you have much more control over how the paint is applied to the model. The tip of the airbrush emits a fine spray of paint. With practice, you can paint a fine, almost pencil–thin line with an airbrush.

An airbrush uses compressed air (and sometimes non–flammable gas) to propel the paint out of the canister and onto your model. You can adjust the flow of the air so that the paint goes on thick or thin. By holding the airbrush just right,

Figure 8–3

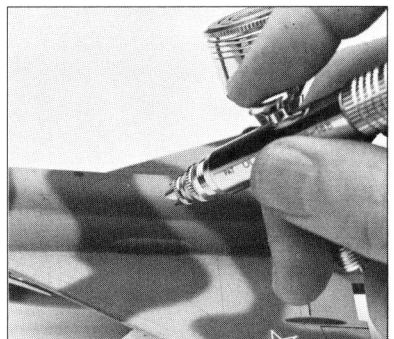

Figure 8–4

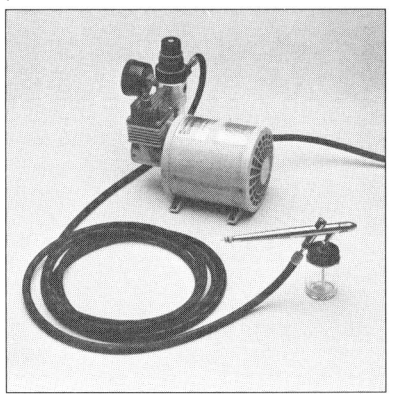

you can obtain all sorts of unique and interesting painting effects, which cannot be duplicated by either spray painting or brush painting.

An airbrush is ideally suited for painting small parts already attached to the model and when painting camouflage colors over the model, as shown in Figure 8–3. These are only two examples of how an airbrush can be used effectively; there are countless others.

The basic airbrush setup consists of the airbrush, a paint bottle (or cup), and an air supply (see Figure 8–4). Hobby airbrushes often use cans of compressed gas as the propellant. (Actually, the cans are filled with a compressed, non–toxic, non–flammable liquid; the liquid vaporizes when it comes out of the can.)

Professional airbrushes use air tanks and compressors.

The air supply is connected to the brush by a hose. You control the air through the brush by pressing a trigger button. When you press down, the air flows through the brush. When you release the button, the air stops. Paint is sucked through the brush when air flows through it.

The paint bottles are removable so you can change colors quickly. To change from red to blue paint, for example, remove the canister filled with red paint and replace it with the one filled with blue paint. The last bit of red paint still in the brush is expelled the moment you push the button. That's why you should always spray the first squirt of paint onto a towel after each color change.

Your airbrush can use paint that comes in bottles, but it must be thinned to the proper consistency first. For best results, a special airbrush thinner should be used. If the paint is too thick, it will clog up the brush. If it is too thin, it won't cover the model well and will be splotchy and unattractive.

Airbrushing is an art, and it takes many hours to get used to it. If you want to learn to use the airbrush, practice first on some scrap artboard. Fill the brush with a color, attach the air supply, and squirt away. Practice holding the brush at just the right angle and be sure to move it back and forth while spraying. Airbrushing is much too involved to be adequately covered in this book. See your library for additional books that offer more details on how to airbrush.

VACUUM–FORMING

Most plastic model kits are made by an injection–molding process. This process is expensive because it requires precision steel molds. In fact, the molds for a single plastic kit can cost well over $100,000. Makers of plastic kits must be sure that enough of their models will sell, or they can't afford to make the molds for them. That means only the most popular cars, ships, airplanes, and other prototypes are made into kits. Yet there are thousands of other prototypes that deserve to be immortalized with a model.

Vacuum–forming is one way to provide kits for unusual models. The molds for vacuum–forming aren't nearly as expensive as those for injection–molding. Some vacuum–formed kits use the same high–impact styrene plastic as the injection– molded kits, so you can assemble them with the same cement, putty, and other supplies. But before building a vacuum–formed kit, read the instructions. If the plastic is not styrene, a special type of cement and putty may be required.

The technique of vacuum–forming is not complicated; in fact, you can do it in your own home. You need a vacuum–forming machine, plastic, and molds. You can even construct your own molds if you can't find what you need. With a vacuum–former, you can build your own models from scratch or replace parts of a kit that have been lost or damaged. See your hobby dealer for more information on vacuum–forming machines.

CONVERSIONS

Some models may not be as accurate as they should be, for example, an airliner that is several inches longer than it should be for its scale. Armed with a saw and a bottle of cement, you can chop up the model and restore the lost authenticity. Or you may want to modify the kit only slightly, to build a model that depicts an earlier version of the prototype.

A conversion means that you take the basic model as presented in the kit and change it here and there as you think necessary. An example of a conversion is shown in Figure 8–5. The model on the left shows the plane as it came from the box. The model on the right shows the conversion.

Converting kits is not extremely difficult, but it does require you to think ahead and to know the kinds of things that are required to make the changes work. If you cut too much from a part, it may not fit with another, and you'll end up throwing your mistakes into the trash.

The basic tools and supplies required for kit conversion are reference materials, a hobby knife, saw, file, sandpaper, and cement or epoxy. An accurate ruler or gauge helps you measure parts; you want to be sure that the parts are the proper scale.

Some conversions entail using parts from other kits. That's why you should always keep the extra parts from models you finish for use in your conversions.

Figure 8–5

Figure 8–6

The average avid model builder has a chest full of extra parts left over from the dozens of models he or she has assembled.

To make it easier to find things fast when you need them, separate your extra parts into categories, such as airplane fuselage parts, tank parts, that sort of thing. Some modeling pros like parts of different scales in separate bins. It's considered taboo, not to mention awkward-looking, to mount a 1/24–scale tank cannon on a 1/72–scale fighter jet.

A few experts use plastic stock for their conversions. The stock is available in various sizes and shapes at the hobby store, like those in Figure 8–6, and is the same styrene plastic used in the kit. You can cut it, saw it, heat it, and cement it to fit your needs. Many conversions are relatively minor, such as:

- Turning the front wheels of a car or truck at an angle

- Making the canopy of an airplane slide back and forth

- Hinging the flaps, ailerons, rudder, and stabilizer in an airplane

- Opening the commander's hatch in a tank.

But some conversions are more complex and require a greater degree of patience and skill:

- Changing a hardtop coupe into a convertible

- Shortening or lengthening the wingspan of an airplane

- Cutting the outer shell of the model to reveal the inner workings, such as a cockpit, engine, or the interior of a submarine

If you are interested in kit conversions, you should practice cutting, filing, and assembling scrap parts. After you get the hang of it, you can attempt your first minor conversions.

BUILDING FROM SCRATCH

Converting models may not be enough for you. Rather, you may want to build something completely new, perhaps an outlandish new interstellar space ship. Your model can be made from plastic stock parts, like those used in conversions, or from extra parts left over from other kits. Imagine an Imperial Battle Cruiser made from extra parts from World War II tank kits!

Scratch–built models can be simple or complex—it's up to you. They can take any shape or form you desire. Many modeling experts construct their own kits as miniatures of something in real life. The airplane in Figure 8–7 shows a scratch-built model built to scale.

Scale modeling means that the size and dimensions of the model must be in direct accord with the prototype. Determining the size of the model requires that you know the dimensions of the real thing, which you can learn from specifications in books and training manuals. Or, if the prototype is nearby, take a tape measure (if the object is small enough) and get the actual dimensions yourself.

Scratch–built models made from your imagination don't have to be so exact or to scale, and they are ideal for first attempts. Before you tackle the immense job of making your own miniature prototype, try assembling a nonscale model from various extra parts and stock plastic. Don't be afraid to cut the parts the size and shape you want. Small parts may be easier to

Figure 8–7

mount if you use tube cement, or better still, 5–minute epoxy.

PRACTICE MAKES PERFECT

Throughout this book, emphasis has been made on rolling up your shirtsleeves and building models. You can't learn model building until you actually try it. If you've been reading this book, but haven't participated in any of the projects, why not start now? Beginning model enthusiasts should try the Snaps–Together model presented in Chapter 1. If you have some experience assembling plastic kits, try the projects in Chapters 2 and 3.

Remember: Practice makes perfect, and in model building, "perfect" means something you can be proud of—now and in the years to come.

Appendix A Testor Cement Drying Chart

Testor Cement Strength*	Time Necessary to Bind Cemented Parts Together	Time Required to Attain Maximum Bond
3501 Cement for Plastic Models	10–15 seconds	2 hours
3502 Plastic Cement (Liquid) (3512, 3516)	15–20 seconds	2 hours
3521 Non-Toxic Cement for Plastic Models (3522, 3523)	20–30 seconds	4 hours
3532 Plastic Model Cement Pen	15–20 seconds	3 hours

*Note: The time period is dependent on a number of variables such as room temperature and humidity, type of mend made, amount of cement used, and quality of the plastic in the model kit.

Appendix B Testor Paint Drying Chart

Testor Coating Type	Print-Free Dry Time (Dry to Touch)
Brushing Gloss Enamels	40–50 minutes
Brushing Flat Enamels	30–40 minutes
Paint Marker Enamels	60–90 minutes
Brushing Clear Lacquers	15–20 minutes
Spray Enamels	15–20 minutes (Gloss and Flat)
Spray Lacquers	8–10 minutes

Note: These drying times represent the time after which painted pieces can be touched and handled without feeling tacky or leaving fingerprints.

These times are based on normal working conditions. As you might expect, the specific drying time for any painted piece depends on a number of factors, including temperature and humidity, the thickness of the coat, the type of plastic painted, the amount of air movement in the work area, and so forth.

It should also be pointed out that Testor enamels are specially formulated with specific drying accelerators (usually referred to as "driers"), which cause the paint film to dry quickly on the top surface, as well as down through the rest of the film. This is the reason print-free drying time is so short for Testor enamels.

However, even though the paint "feels" dry, the paint film is still curing. For this reason, you should always let the painted model sit undisturbed overnight. After a full 6 to 12 hours of drying, the pieces can be cemented and handled normally. You should wait 24 hours before sanding, washing, or repainting.

Subject Index

A

Action figures
    adding to cars, 88
    adding to military vehicles, 93-94
    painting, 95-96
Action models, 85-96
    aircraft, 94-95
    cars, 87-90
    military vehicles, 90-94
    painting action figures for, 95-96
Adzing, 44-45
Airbrushing, 114-116
Aircraft
    action models of, 94-95
    camouflage painting of, 70-74
    detailing canopies and canopy frames of, 67-69
    detailing engine of, 70
    detailing tires of, 69
    painting cockpit of, 65-66
    painting landing gear of, 66

    ready to go, 94-95
    weathering, 74-80, 95
Alignment pins. See Locating pins
Assembly, aids in, 30-31

B

Backgrounds for models
    color, 104-105
    dioramas for, 105
    photographs and posters for, 104-105
    scale stands and bases for, 102-104
Bases. See also Stands (display)
    scale background, 102-104
Bottle paint, 7, 8-10, 41. See also Brush painting; Paint; Painting models
    applying, 9
    cleaning up, 10
    drying, 9-10
    drying time for, 122
    handling, 8-9
    thinning, 42, 43
Brush. See Paint brush

Brush painting, 40-43. See also Bottle paints; Painting models models
    brush sizes for, 41
    for camouflaging, 71-72
    changing colors, 42
    cleaning up after, 42-43
    for touch up, 47
Bubbling of decals, 28
Building your own model, 119-120

C

Camouflaging techniques, 70-74, 92
    brush painting, 71
    masking, 72-73
    sponge painting, 71
    stencils for, 73-74
Cars
    action models of, 87-90
    adding action figures to, 88
    detailing, 88-90
    opening hood and trunk of, 87-88
    turning wheels on, 87,118